Learning Islam through Stories

Introduces Islam through Islamic history, personalities, events, and stories. The course will also introduce worship rituals, religious festivals, practices, and various supplications taught by the Prophet Muhammad (peace be upon him).

Publisher: Ghamidi Center of Islamic Learning - Al-Mawrid US
ISBN: 978-1-966600-24-4

Address: 3620 N Josey Ln, Suite 230 Carrollton, TX 75007
Website: www.ghamidicenter.com
Email: info@ghamidi.org

Chapter 1

Introduction to the course

This chapter introduces the course and its topics.

Introduction

This course aims to build a strong foundation for children learning about Islam for the very first time in a classroom setting. The course introduces Islam through Islamic history, personalities, events, and stories. For younger ages, this is the most effective method for introducing concepts such as God, prophets, creation, and many others, including ethics, morals, human attitudes, values, and cultural norms and differences. Also, through historical Islamic events and the life stories of the mighty prophets of Islam, the course will introduce worship rituals, religious festivals, practices, and various supplications taught by Prophet Muhammad (peace be upon him). The course will specifically train children to understand, discuss, appreciate, and apply the key messages and morals behind these historical events and stories, and to evaluate their daily lives in light of this learning.

Course Objectives

- Narrate the stories of the lives of the Prophets in Islam.
- Understand the wisdom behind stories and how to benefit from them.
- Understand and narrate various stories from the Quran.
- Memorize and recite Prophetic Duas.
- Understand worship rituals, their pillars, and the wisdom behind them.
- Perform their religious rituals correctly, e.g., ablution and prayer.
- Memorize and recite the utterances in prayer.
- Learn about religious festivals and their rituals, e.g., Eid and animal sacrifice.

Topics covered in the course

We will learn about Islam through learning about the following:

1 Islamic History

4 Islamic Personalities

2 Events of the Past

5 Islamic Practices

3 The world around us

Concepts and Learning Process

During this course, we will learn the following concepts. Some of them we already know, but some might be new. However, we will learn it together.

These are the different tools that we will use to learn Islam.

You will go over the content that we have created for you

You will be asked a question, and you will discuss it as a group and learn together

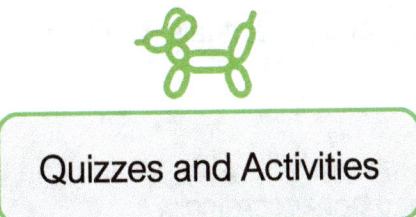

The class will do an activity together or be given as an assignment to individual students

The Quran and Stories

Why does the Quran have so many stories?

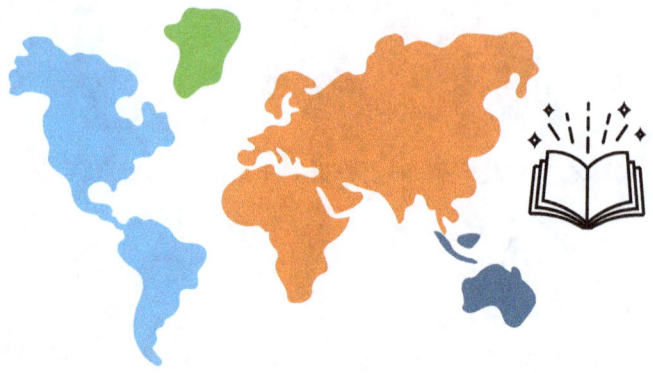

- We call them stories, but these are actual events from the past.
- Stories or events are the best way to learn about something and remember it.
- They help us understand different situations that people have been put through in the past.
- These stories also help us understand how people react in these situations and what lessons they teach us.
- The Quran uses them as a reminder to us when we face similar situations.

The Goals of the Course

- Learn the foundation (basis) of Islam.
- Learn the stories of the prophets.
- Understand the wisdom behind these stories.
- Memorize (know by heart) the duas of the prophets.
- Understand worship practices and the wisdom behind them.
- Understand the pillars (units) of Islam.
- Learn about religious festivals and their rituals (worship).

Lessons we can learn

We must compare the Quranic stories with our situation and use their wisdom (lessons) to change our lives and act accordingly.

Important notes

- Throughout the course, the words "God" and "Allah" are used interchangeably.
- For brevity and editing, the salutations for the Prophet Muhammad, PEACE BE UPON HIM, are not repeated when his name comes. But it is highly encouraged that whenever we say or read his name, we send him salutations.

Class instructions

- You are required to attend all classes unless you have a valid reason to skip.
- Please send a note (or ask your parents) to your teacher on Google Classroom if you will skip a session.
- Attendance will be taken at the beginning of every class. Arriving in class 5 minutes after the start will be counted as tardy.
- Three (3) tardies will be counted as one absence.
- Attendance will be counted toward your final assessment.
- Every student will be assessed via:
  - Participation in the class
  - Multiple Quizzes
  - Assignments
  - Semester Exam
  - End-of-Year Exam

Chapter 2

What is Islam?

This chapter introduces Islam briefly, including its beliefs and pillars.

Understanding Islam

Definition

> Submitting our will to the Will of Allah under all situations

They are Muslim

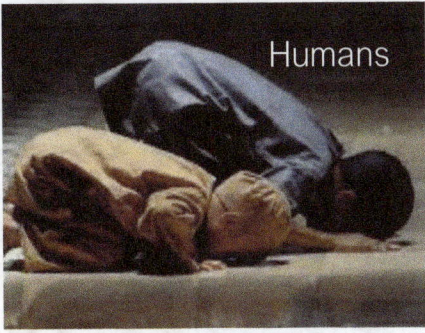

We are Muslim

- Other creatures submit to Allah through natural laws. For example, the Sun always shines, and trees grow and benefit humans, as commanded.
- Similarly, we are asked to submit our will to Allah. These creatures do not have a choice, but we do. That's why our Islam has more value in the eyes of Allah.
- When we submit to Allah with a full heart, we are called Muslims. A Muslim is someone who submits to Allah.

Pillars of Islam

- Think of Islam as a building. A building stands on its pillars. If the pillars break, the building falls down.
- Similarly, Islam's foundation, or pillars, are important.

Shahadah or Declaration of Faith	Salah or Prayers five times a da	Zakah or Charity once a year	Saum or Fasting during Ramadan	Hajj or Pilgrimage to Makkah once in a lifetime

A MISUNDERSTANDING

> Most Muslims think Islam's main goal is to believe and practice the five pillars (main units) of Islam.

The Building of Islam

- Now, let's look at the building of Islam and how it should be built from the ground up.

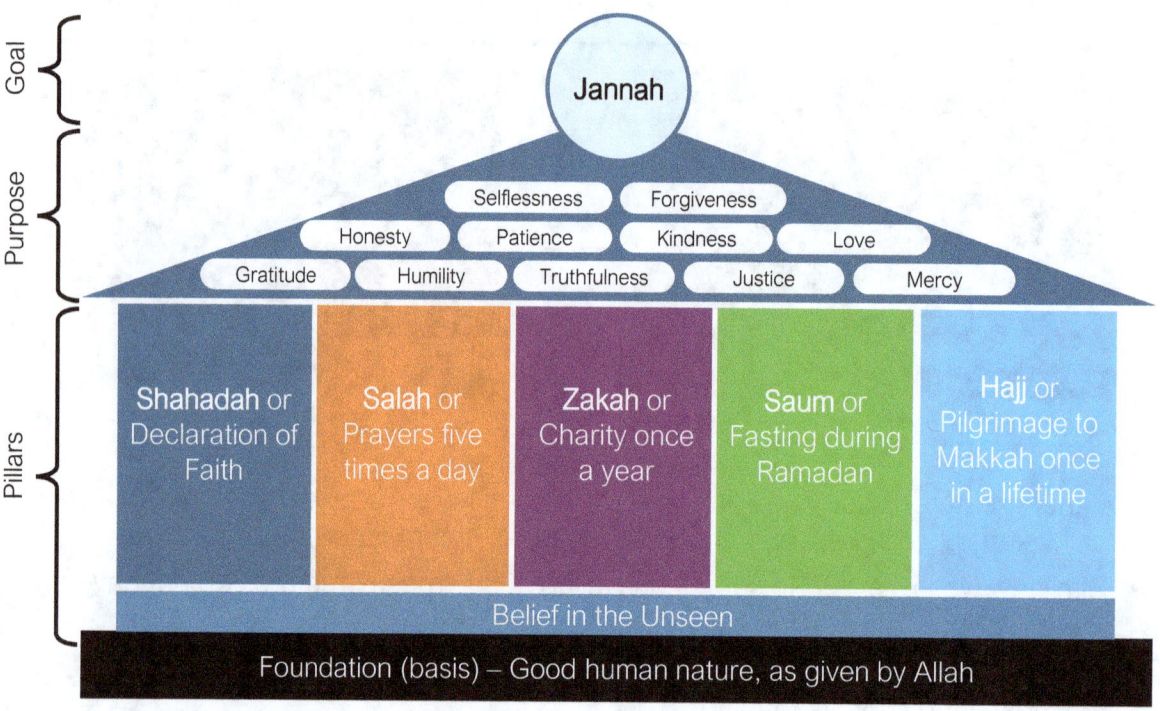

- Everyone has the foundation of good human nature.
- We believe in certain beliefs that are very close to our human nature. For example, we all want to believe in a powerful God or be rewarded for the good work we do.
- Our beliefs result in certain practices, which form the pillars. For e.g., if we believe in life after death, then we should help our fellow human beings or worship God.
- Good human nature, belief in a powerful God, and Islamic practices must develop noble character values in us. That is the real purpose of Islam.
- This leads us to the ultimate goal of Jannah.
- Remember, pillars are not buildings; they only support buildings.

Do you know what Muslims believe in?

Our Beliefs

- Belief is the acceptance in your heart and the verbal statement that something is true or exists.
- Our beliefs are centered on Allah. Which means if one does not believe in Allah, no other belief is valid.
- Our actions and practices depend on our beliefs.
- When we believe in Allah, we believe in Him with all of His attributes. For example, He is All-Powerful, All-Seeing, All-Hearing, All-Knowing, etc.

- There is one God, and He is our Creator. None shares His Lordship (As a King).

- He chooses a few people and talks with them to give guidance.

- He also gives His guidance in writing in the form of Divine (from God) Books.

- A creation made of light obeys Him and performs many duties in this world.

- All humanity will be asked for their beliefs and acts ONE Day

The Quran only mentions these 5 articles of Faith. There is another article, "Fate," mentioned in the Hadith, which falls under the belief in Allah.

Muslim

1. **Testimony (Shahada)** – It is a simple statement: "I bear witness there is no God but Allah, and Muhammad is His servant and messenger". It's called the Declaration of Faith. If someone wants to become a Muslim, they should recite this in their heart or in front of other people (preferred).

Ashadul Un La ILAHA ILLA Allah Wa Ashadu Anna
Muhammadan Abdaho wa Rasooluhu

You firmly state that there is no God we should worship except Allah. You also firmly state that Prophet Muhammad is the Messenger and Servant of Allah. All other beliefs (prophets, angels, books, day of judgment, fate) are included in this statement. If we agree that Prophet Muhammad is a true Prophet, then he has given us the Quran. The Quran told us that Allah has created Angels, He has sent Prophets before Prophet Muhammad with Books, there will be a Day of Judgment, and Allah controls everything.

2. **Prayer (Salah)** – We pray five times a day: at dawn, noon, afternoon, sunset, and night.

3. **Charity (Zakat)** – We are asked to share what we are given by Allah. Every year, those who have enough money give a small portion (2.5%) of their savings to help people in need, such as the poor or sick.

4. **Fasting (Sawm)** – Once a year, during the special month of Ramadan, healthy adults and older kids fast from dawn to dusk, during which they do not eat or drink.

5. **Pilgrimage (Hajj)** – Once in their lifetime, if we are healthy and can afford it, Muslims travel to the city of Makkah in Saudi Arabia in the month of Dhul Hijjah. Millions of people from every country in the world gather there to perform Hajj as one big family.

We will learn about each of them later in the course.

Why is it better to recite this statement in front of other people, like a crowd in the mosque of your community?

The concept of fate

- Before we conclude, let's talk about Fate, also known as Qadr in Arabic.
- It is not a separate belief but part of the belief in Allah, because if we believe that Allah is the true God, then He created everything and knows everything that has happened to us.

What is Fate?

- Qadr means that Allah knows everything about the past, present, and future, including our lives, and it's all written in a Big Book.
- It also means a few things that He has decided for us, over which we have no control. For example, what kind of talent will you be born with?

But ……

- That does not mean we are robots. Allah's knowledge about everything does not affect our choices in life. We still know what is good and bad. Don't you?

Examples from this world

- **Example 1:** When playing a video game, the game designer has programmed all the moves, but you still make your own choices. No forcing!

- **Example 2:** A GPS has all the routes to every destination, but it does not control your drive. You are free to choose wherever you want to go. You may end up at the wrong location.

Activity

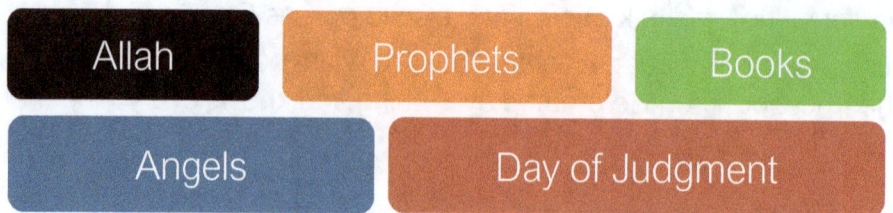

Read the sentences below and fill in the right color in the circles according to the belief that the statement refers to.

○ Prophet Muhammad is the Final Messenger of Allah.

○ Jesus is not the son of God but a mighty Prophet.

○ The Quran is the True word of Allah.

○ We should not commit injustice to anyone.

○ Angel Jibrael used to bring the Quran to Prophet Muhammad.

○ This world will end.

○ No one can help us on the Day of Judgment.

○ The Bible has a lot of wisdom.

○ At the time of death, our soul is taken.

○ Allah knows even what's in our hearts.

○ Good Muslims will live in Paradise forever.

Why is belief in Allah at the center of everything?

Activity

Instructions

- In turn, a child should count continuously from 1 to 5.
- A second child should be assigned to call a STOP to stop the child at random while the first child is counting from 1 to 5
- Whichever number the first stop, he/she will be asked to state one fact about that belief.

Example

- If the first child stops at number 5, he/she has to tell one fact about the Day of Judgment. For example, "we don't know when the Day of Judgment will come."

Activity

Instructions:

1. Put these pictures in the faith bucket that is most appropriate or related.
2. Think hard to see the relationship.
3. One picture per child, and then take turns.
4. The teacher should ask the children about each picture until all the pictures are finished.

Chapter 3

The Story of Creation

In this chapter, we will learn the story of our creation as described in the Quran.

Our Creator, Allah

- There is no doubt that we are created beings, and every created being has a creator. For example, when we see a picture, the first thing we want to know is who painted it.
- **Allah** is our Creator and the Creator of everything.
- He also maintains our lives and everything in this universe.
- Over billions of years, Allah created the stars, planets, moons, and galaxies.
- Allah created the laws of nature that govern the universe.
- Allah created life in many places throughout the universe, not just on Earth.

How do we know Allah?

✔ Allah has no form that we can see nor any shape we can imagine.

✔ He told us in the Quran that "nothing is like Him."

✔ It would be very difficult for us to imagine what Allah is since there are no details we can imagine.

✔ The best way to understand Allah is by understanding his qualities. We have some of those qualities to a certain extent (generous, kind, patient, etc.).

✔ Some of his attributes are:

The Compassionate	The Most Merciful	The Just
The Wise	The Grateful	The Reckoner
The Mighty	The Protector	The Great

His creations

- Allah created this universe and three unique creations that we will discuss.

What does the Quran say about the Universe?

- Allah created this universe way before He created us.
- Allah created the universe in six Stages (The Quran used the word Al-Yaum, which means days, period, or stages).
- Allah made the stars, planets, moons, and galaxies.
- Although the Quran did not talk about it, it took billions of years to reach the stage at which humans were created.

It is important to note that the Quran is not a book of science; it is a book of guidance, and it discusses scientific facts only when it delves deeply into creation.

How did we reach here?

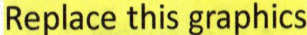

- Earth had water everywhere in the beginning.
- Allah created living things on this Earth, including tiny organisms, plants, fish, amphibians, lizards, and, much later, dinosaurs.
- Allah created man from the elements of the Earth.
- Humans we know today did not evolve into a species (form) from another species (form).

Source: Propel Steps

- Allah created every species in its original form.
- Every species undergoes evolutionary change (things improve over time in response to the environment).
- The first intelligent human on Earth was Adam. There may be human-like species before Adam, but the Quran is silent on the matter.

Many scientists suggest that we were not created but evolved from animals. Do you know what that scientific theory is called?

Human Beings

- The first unique creation is human beings, us. We are made of clay from this earth.
- Allah gave us the ability to think and make decisions – we are free to choose.
- We are intelligent and can think about the world around us and understand it.
- We have feelings like love, hate, passion, etc.
- The first intelligent human beings on earth were Adam and his wife. All human beings came from Adam and his wife. That makes all of us brothers and sisters in humanity.

Angels

- Angels are made of light; they can assume human form. Angels are not male or female.
- They do whatever Allah tells them to do – workers of Allah.
- Allah does not need helpers, but He made angels to show us that things happen through the means He provides.
- All angels are good; they are present with Him all the time.
- They only appear to Prophets and Messengers to give them messages from Allah.
- They may appear before us, but we have no way of knowing.

Jinns

- Jinn (which means "hidden") is made of fire energy. We cannot see them, but they can see us.
- They are born, they live, then they die.
- Good Jinns keep to themselves and do not interfere in human affairs.
- Bad Jinns -- also called devils or "Shayateen"-- bother us by whispers (speaking quietly) of evil thoughts into our minds; they do not force us to do wrong.
- Allah wants humans to ignore and avoid Jinns because they want to ruin humans and their good hearts.
- People who try to contact Jinns become slaves of Jinns, doing bad deeds and committing sins.

What do you think is more powerful among humans, angels, and Jinns?

Humans are different

- We share many qualities with animals. For example, both humans and animals feel hunger.
- But there are three things that differentiate human beings from animals and other creatures

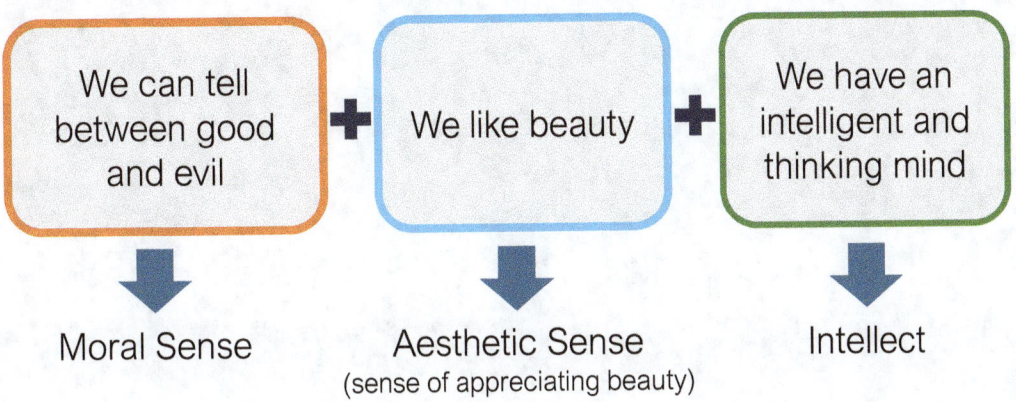

Lessons Learned

- If we are created beings, then there must be a Creator for us.
- Allah does not create things and make them appear magically. Everything goes through a process.
- Allah is Kind, Compassionate, and Merciful. He created life and everything we need in this world.
- Our moral behavior is one of the reasons we are different from other creatures.
- Shaytan tells us reasons to feel good about our evil deeds and actions; he wants us to go to Hell.
- If we plan to do good, Angels help us in that plan. If we plan to do evil, Shaytan helps us with that plan after we receive the warning from within us.

Activity

- Pick a planet/star other than ours and write 6-10 facts about it.
- Write 5-10 key points about the scientific theory called the Theory of Evolution.

Chapter 4

The Story of the Two Worlds

In this chapter, we will learn about the two worlds that Allah talked about in the Quran. One of them we live in, and another one will be created later.

Our Life as Planned by Allah

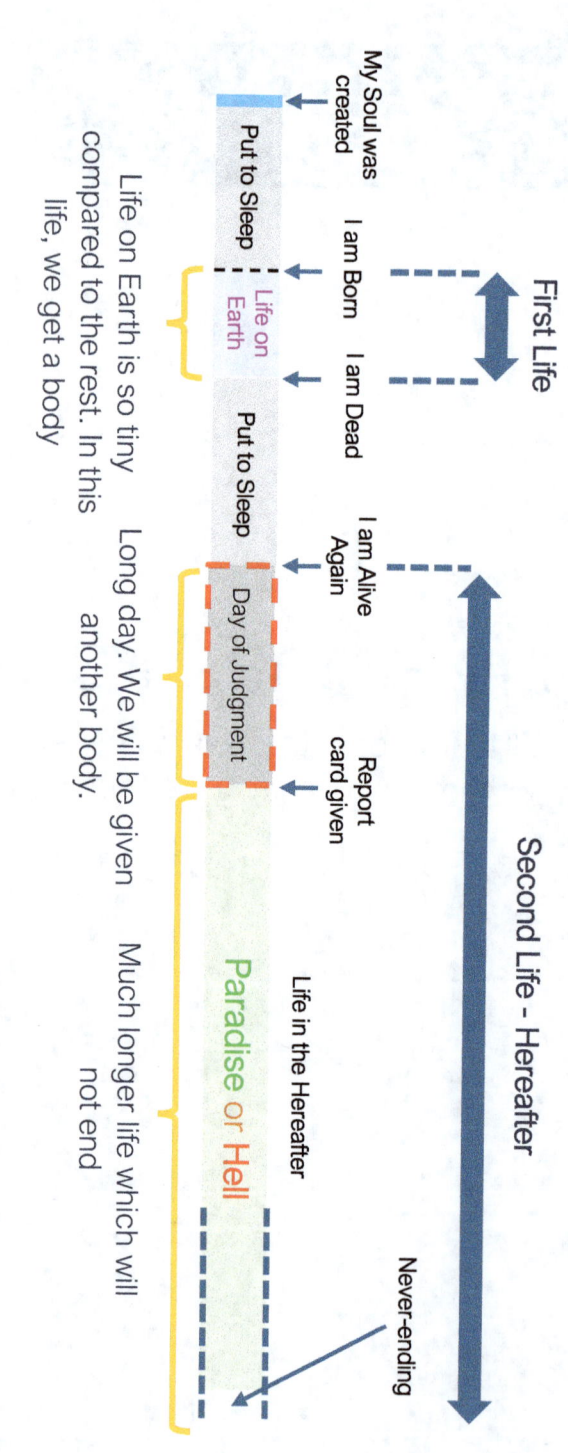

Two Worlds

- Allah created us with a plan and a purpose. Our lives and deaths are not random but part of a larger plan.
- Allah planned two Worlds for us, and we live in the first one. After this one, He will create another, much larger one. Every human being will live in both Worlds.

Life on Earth (First world)

- If we look at our complete life as planned by Allah, this is the shortest part of life.
- Allah creates our life in the wombs of our mothers.
- In the order (under normal situations):
  - We are born
  - Normally, children grow into adults
  - We reach a certain age and die
- We have control over some things and none over others. For example, we never chose our place of birth.
- We control our behavior, intentions, feelings, goals, desires, and motivations (what we want to do).

Freedom to choose (Free Will)

- Most of the time, we know what is right and what is wrong.
- In this life, we choose our actions and reactions.
- We face different situations every moment of our lives. Some are under our control, and some are not.

- We are given opportunities (positive openings) and challenges to improve ourselves.
- We choose whether to learn from our experience.
- Sometimes, we see the results of choosing right or wrong in this world. But mostly we will see the results in the second world.
- In every situation, Allah wants us to choose right and avoid wrong.

Name any two things in our lives that we do not have any control over?

The Expected Result

- Our actions in the first life or world will determine our results in the second world.
- All our words and actions in this world are recorded by the angels appointed for this task.
- Before we get the results, we will be asked questions about our behavior in this world, and our records will be shown to us.
- As in a court of law, Allah will decide our results, and then we will either go to Heaven or Hell, depending on the results.

We see both paths clearly in this world

Bad in the end

Wrong   Right

Good in the end

- Sometimes we are confused or not aware of something. If you cannot decide on something, always ask someone older and wiser than you!
- The bad results of a wrong decision or act may not appear in this world, but in the Hereafter, it will be bad if not corrected in this life.
- What matters is the end result in the next world. We may see that the bad deeds we committed here did not have any negative results.
- If we realize at any time that we have done wrong, we should correct it immediately and ask Allah's forgiveness, and the wrong will be cleared from our records.

Do you feel bad when you do something wrong?

The Day of Judgment

The end of the first world

- This world will end abruptly in the middle of a routine day.
- Angel Israfeel will blow the trumpet (big horn).
- Horrible, terrifying (scary) events will occur worldwide. The Earth will be destroyed in an abnormal tragedy.
- Every human being alive at that time will instantly die when the horn blows.
- A new world will be created after that, and we will be alive again.

Source: Live Science

Deeds will be the currency of the Day of Judgment

- When we die, our soul is separated from our body, and we are put to sleep.
- A new world will be created for the next life. That is called the Hereafter.
- We will wake up from a long sleep on this Day.
- Allah will recreate people for this Day – they will be given a new body.

- ALL of humanity will stand for judgment and results.
- Everyone will be sorted into groups based on different factors.
- The most important factor would be the belief in Allah, our Creator.
- The best of the people (front-runners), good people (2nd best), and bad people.
- Similar to money, people will exchange deeds based on situations.

Do you ever wonder why the universe is so huge, and humans live on such a tiny planet?

Book of Deeds

Remember, Angels write everything we say or do when we are alive in this world.

- Each person will be shown a record of what he or she did while they were alive.
- Nothing will be hidden. Even our body parts will speak against us!
- We will be asked about our beliefs and deeds.
- The good and the evil deeds will be weighed and measured.
- Based on the result (which one is heavier), we will be assigned to our final place (Paradise or Hell).
- If we have wronged someone and have not asked for forgiveness from that person in this world, it will be settled on that day.
- However, our good intentions will count, and Allah may forgive us if we make mistakes while always wanting to do good.

وَ اِنَّ عَلَيْكُمْ لَحٰفِظِيْنَ ۙ كِرَامًا كَاتِبِيْنَ ۙ يَعْلَمُوْنَ مَا تَفْعَلُوْنَ

Indeed, appointed over you are guardians, very noble writers; they know what you do. (82:10-12)

اِذْ يَتَلَقَّى الْمُتَلَقِّيٰنِ عَنِ الْيَمِيْنِ وَ عَنِ الشِّمَالِ قَعِيْدٌ

مَا يَلْفِظُ مِنْ قَوْلٍ اِلَّا لَدَيْهِ رَقِيْبٌ عَتِيْدٌ

They should remember when two takers are seated to their right and left; not a word does a person say, but there is a vigilant guardian next to him. (50:17-18)

Life in the Hereafter – Forever

- After a long Day of Judgment, the results will be announced.
- People who will be successful will be given their results in their right hands. They will go to Paradise and will live there forever.
- People who will fail will be given their results in their left hands. They will go to Hell and live there forever or until Allah wants them to be in.
- Allah will forgive many people based on their intentions and shortcomings.
- Remember, Hell is Allah's warning, and Paradise is Allah's promise, and Allah never breaks His promise.

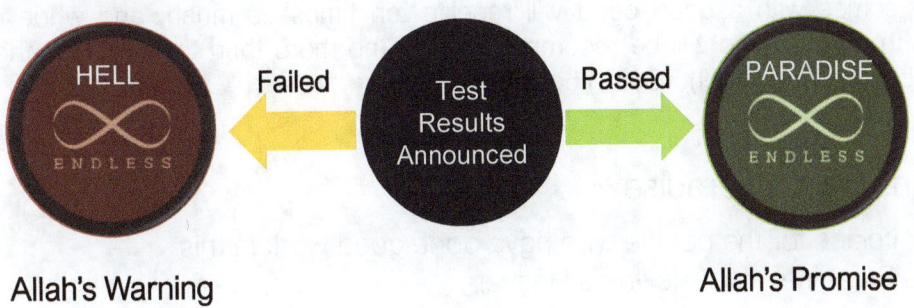

Allah's Warning   Allah's Promise

إِنَّ اللهَ لَا يُخْلِفُ الْمِيعَادَ

In fact, Allah never breaks His promise

Relationship between two worlds (lives)

| Life on Earth | The two lives are connected | Life in Hereafter |

What to do:

- Know who your Creator is and be grateful to Him.
- When doing something wrong, stop and think twice.
- Be good to others and help them.
- Always side with the truth.
- Avoid bad company.
- Don't be mean and nasty to others
- Always look at your deeds and think about what you are doing and what needs correction.

Allah does not want us to fail

- Remember! Allah is the Most Merciful and Most Generous, and He does not want us to fail on the Day of Judgment.
- Because of His generosity, He only counts 1 bad deed (if minor sin) when we do bad, but He counts 10 or more good deeds when we do good.
- This means if we always try to be good but make mistakes sometimes, we can never fail on the Day of Judgment and never end up in Hell.

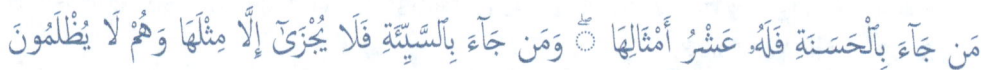

Whoever comes with a good deed will receive **ten times** as much, and whoever comes with an evil deed will be recompensed with no more than the like, and they shall not be wronged (at all). (Quran 6:160)

What is in Heaven/Paradise?

- The final place for the people who have done good work in this world is Paradise, also known as Heaven.
- They will live in Paradise forever.
- The rewards will be similar to what we enjoy in this life, but much, much better and more. You can wish for whatever you want.
- We will be able to see Allah.
- No problems, no sickness, no troubles! There will be no concept of death.

What is in Hell?

- There will be various types of punishments and tortures for the body and soul.
- The most severe will be burning in the fire.
- For example, burning by fire, boiling water to drink, dry, nasty food to eat, chained, choking smoke, and fire.
- Severe punishment will be for arrogant (proud) people who were wicked (evil) in this life and will be in it forever.
- Sinful people will be punished, but eventually taken out of hell and sent to paradise.

Lessons Learned

- Every living thing will die one day.
- Everyone will be held accountable for everything they have done in their lives.
- If someone is not punished for a bad deed, that does not mean Allah will never ask.
- It is up to us and Allah's Mercy where we will end up – Paradise or Hell.
- After we die, we will all be brought back to life before Allah.
- Our records will be shown to us, and nothing will be hidden.
- In Paradise, we can do whatever we want, including seeing Allah.
- In Hell, we will be punished for our evil deeds.

Live in this world, enjoy it with a focus on the Hereafter

Activity

Make a deed chart for yourself for one week. Write/Count every deed you do. Give 10 marks to all good ones and 1 mark to bad ones. Tell us your total in the end (positive or negative). If you are not sure about a deed, whether it is good or bad, ask your parents or teacher.

Chapter 5

The Grand Test

In this chapter, we will learn about the grand test that we are all in. This will help us understand the nature of our life.

Do you know what a test is?

The Journey of Life

Life is a test

- If you know the concept of a test, you will understand this life as well.
- This world is a factory of life (people come) and death (people leave). People are born and die every day.
- Allah created every human being for Paradise, but He wants us to earn it after passing a test in this life, because life in Paradise will be amazing and cannot be given to everyone.
- Life on Earth is short-lived. The test is always short, but the results are long-lasting.
- That's why this life is a TEST.
- The duration of the next life is much longer than our current life, and it will be a reward for this life, good or bad.
- For example, when you see a $10 bill dropped by one of your friends, and they did not notice, it is your test to make the right decision and do the right thing: pick it up and give it to the owner.
- Similarly, we are tested multiple times every day, and our deeds are recorded for counting on the Day of Judgment.
- Our test starts when we are old enough to make decisions.

 During testing, we must act responsibly while still having fun.

Being a Muslim does not mean you cannot have fun. Enjoy your life responsibly with a focus on the Hereafter. Moderation (middle way) is key. Avoid extremes.

The Nature of Allah's Creations & the Grand Test

Nature of Creations

- Every creation of Allah has a nature they are born with.
- Allah has given humans, angels, and Jinn freedom to choose their actions and whether to obey Him.
- Angels obey Allah and carry out His orders because they are always with Him (although it is unclear whether they see Him). There may or may not be a test for them.
- Humans and Jinns are in the test because of this freedom to choose their actions.
- Allah created humans and Jinn to live their lives according to His rules; they are born with all the good qualities to follow them.

Human Nature

- Humans have been created with many good qualities – self-awareness (knowing yourself), intelligence, kindness, goodwill (ability to favor), patience, love, and compassion.
- Humans also have weaknesses:
  - Forget things easily
  - We act selfishly
  - Want quick results – impatient
- These two competing qualities act on ALL of us (good and bad).
- Everyone's basic nature is good – no one is born evil.
- The real test is to overcome these weaknesses with qualities and always try to do good.

Nature of Jinn

- They were created before us. They live with us in this world, but we have very little knowledge about them.
- They have families like us. We cannot see them, but they can see us.
- There are good and bad Jinn.
- They have prophets and messengers like us.
- Some of them are arrogant, which leads to disobedience of Allah.
- Their interaction with humans is minimal.
- They prefer to live in places far from the human population.

Satan (Shaytan) – Devil

- Shaytan (Satan) is an adjective that can be applied to humans and Jinn. But we usually associate them with Jinn.
- One of them, Iblees, misguided Adam and Eve, and they made a mistake because of him.
- When Allah got angry with him, he promised Allah that he would misguide good people.
- They attempt to mislead us into becoming selfish, arrogant, and dishonest.
- They have no control over us, but they misguide us through small thoughts, whispers, an urge, an emotion, and more.
- Some human beings become friends of Shaytan. Beware!
- When you do bad, Shaytan suggests, "It is OK because ......"

Our focus should be on defeating Shaytan's plans.

Allah's Grand Test

- Allah wanted to create a permanent (long) life for us, but He wanted to test us by giving us a temporary (short) life.
- Our actions in this life determine what kind of life we will have in the Hereafter.
- Passing the Test means rewards in the Hereafter.
- Failing the Test means punishment in the Hereafter.
- Those who lack faith in Allah, act without morals, and do evil deeds reach a place of suffering.
- Those who have good faith in Allah, act morally and do good deeds, reach a place of bliss.
- When you leave this world, you only take your Faith and a record of your deeds with you – everything else will remain here.

Discuss a few situations when you think you are being tested by Allah.

What are we tested with?

- Every day, we are tested with one of these or both: Being Thankful or Being Patient.
- Allah sees how we behave in these situations. Everyone is tested without exception.
- We face situations in which we are sometimes tested for gratitude and, in others, for patience. Some examples are given below.

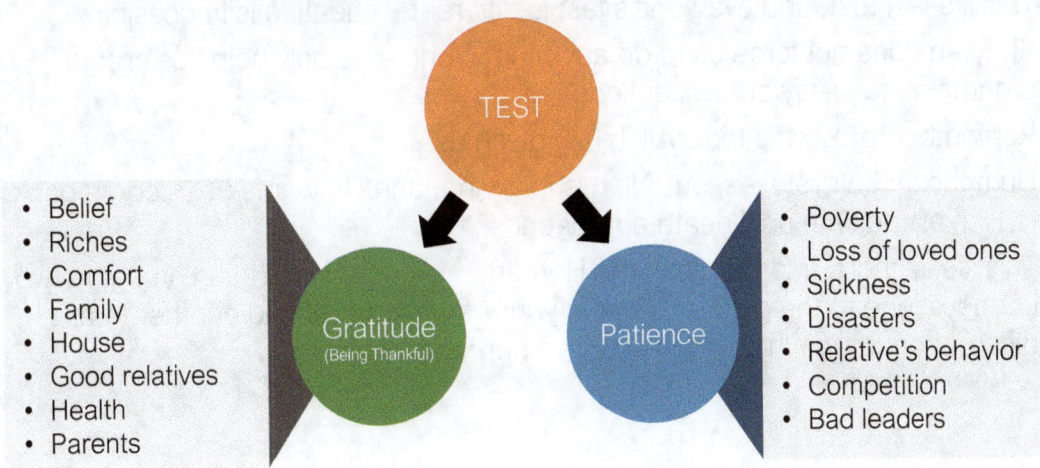

- Belief
- Riches
- Comfort
- Family
- House
- Good relatives
- Health
- Parents

- Poverty
- Loss of loved ones
- Sickness
- Disasters
- Relative's behavior
- Competition
- Bad leaders

Tools given to us to pass the test

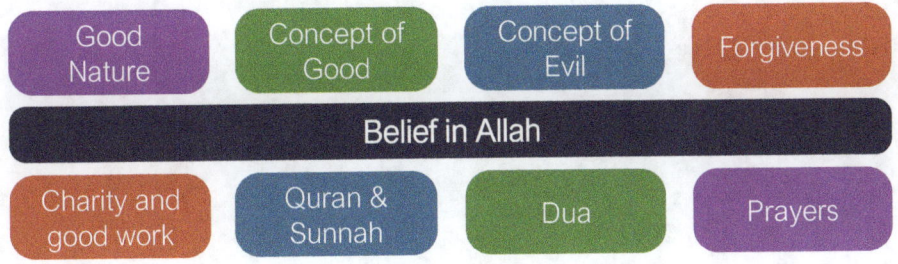

- Allah is Merciful, and He wants us to pass the test.
- Allah has sent the Quran to us, which contains everything that we must believe in to help us pass this test.
- It also contains an entire moral code of life that will help us pass this test.
- He gave this final message of guidance through the Prophet Muhammad, who personally conveyed it to humanity.
- Prophet Muhammad's life and teachings are the best examples for us to follow (Seerah and Hadith).
- Look, how Merciful Allah is!

Lessons Learned

- Lead your life in the best possible manner; enjoy it, but do not lose sight of the Hereafter.
- If we know this life is temporary, why risk ending up in the wrong place in the Hereafter?
- This life is a test, and everyone's test is different – cheating is impossible.
- Shaytan does not force us to do anything wrong – he only helps us create arguments to justify our evil actions.
- Remember to use the tools Allah has given us.
- Humans make mistakes, but Allah is forgiving, and He wants us to come back to Him all the time until death approaches.
- This life is short, and the life in the Hereafter is longer in duration. Imagine two journeys: one to the grocery store in your neighborhood and another to a different country. Which journey will you prepare more for?

Chapter 6

The Story of Prophet Adam

In this chapter, we will learn about the story of Prophet Adam, which has been mentioned in the Quran many times.

Why do Prophets come?

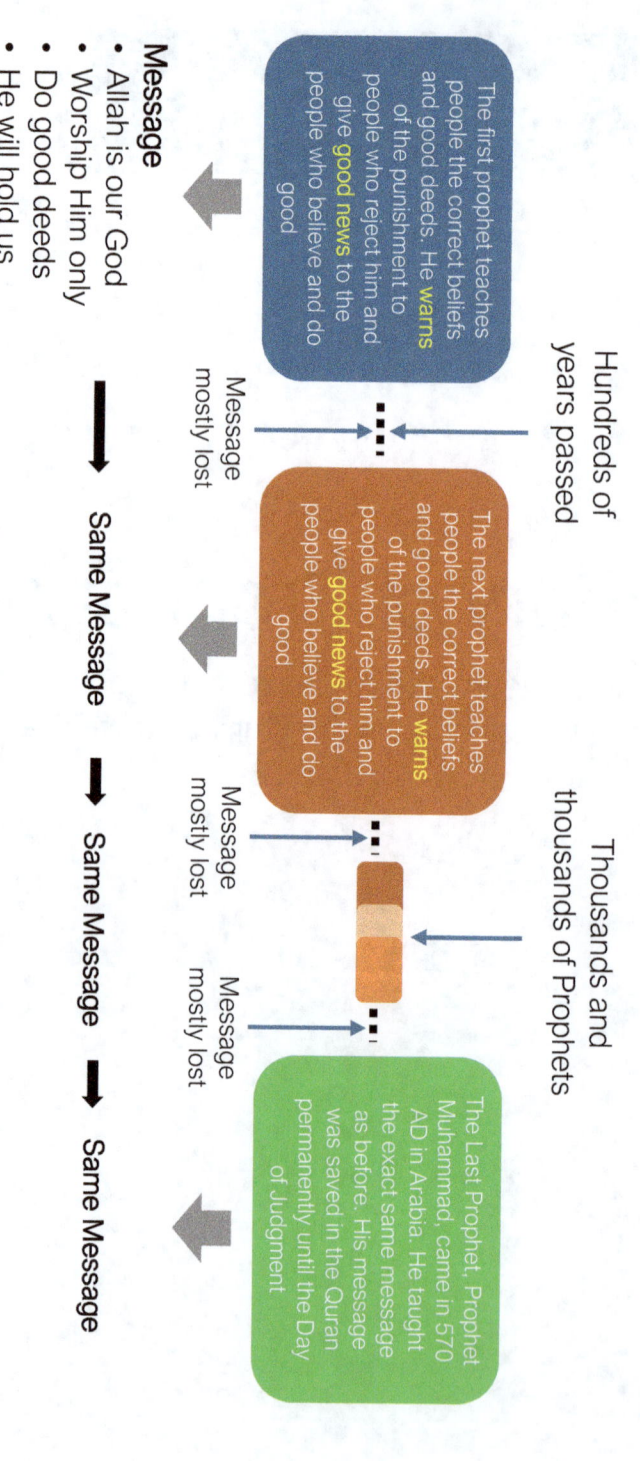

The first prophet teaches people the correct beliefs and good deeds. He warns of the punishment to people who reject him and give good news to the people who believe and do good

Hundreds of years passed

Message mostly lost

The next prophet teaches people the correct beliefs and good deeds. He warns of the punishment to people who reject him and give good news to the people who believe and do good

Thousands and thousands of Prophets

Message mostly lost

Message mostly lost

The Last Prophet, Prophet Muhammad, came in 570 AD in Arabia. He taught the exact same message as before. His message was saved in the Quran permanently until the Day of Judgment

Same Message

Same Message

Same Message

Message
- Allah is our God
- Worship Him only
- Do good deeds
- He will hold us accountable for our deeds

Prophet Adam

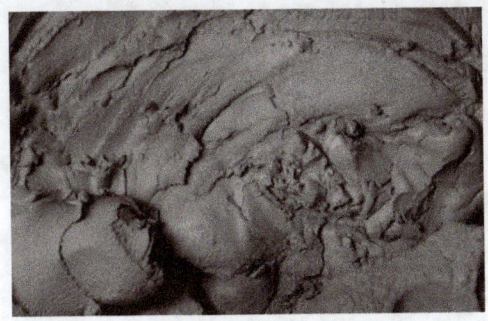

وَلَقَدْ خَلَقْنَا ٱلْإِنسَٰنَ مِن صَلْصَٰلٍ مِّنْ حَمَإٍ مَّسْنُونٍ

Indeed, We created humans from sounding clay molded from black mud. (Al-Hijr 26)

- Allah created human beings out of clay. It could mean that, initially, human beings were born of clay.
- When He perfected them, He chose Adam and Eve as the first humans (intelligent ones), blessed them with unique features that earlier humans lacked.
- Allah blew His special soul into them (that's what makes us special in this world).
- Allah told the angels He had created Adam:
  - His children will be caretakers of this Earth
  - He and his children would rule over Earth with power
  - They will remain on Earth for some time and will be tested
- First, they feared that humans would cause problems because they would have power, but then Allah told them the full scheme, and they agreed.
- He asked the angels and the jinn to bow down to Adam.
- It was a test from Allah for both of them.

A test for Angels and Jinn

- Both Angels and Jinns are more powerful than humans. It was a big test for them to obey Allah. They obeyed Allah because He is their Creator and our Master.
- Iblees (Shaytan) did not obey because he was arrogant. Arrogance blinds people, and they cannot see the truth.

Angels' and Most of the good Jinns' Response

YES

Humble and Obedient

Iblees (one of the Jinns) Response

NO

Arrogant and Disobedient

Adam and Shaytan

Satan was disgraced

- Allah had decided to disgrace (shame) Shaytan due to his:
    - Defiance (Refusal to accept)
    - Arrogance
    - The choice to go against the order of Allah on purpose
- Shaytan would not receive the Mercy of Allah in this world.
- On the day of Judgment, Shaytan would be an outcast (rejected).

Shaytan Challenge

- Shaytan asked Allah for some time until the Day of Judgement so he could mislead man – Allah granted him the time he asked for.
- Shaytan said he would make immorality and evil seem good to human beings – he promised to corrupt all of mankind morally.
- Humans would follow the straight path that leads them back to Allah and His Paradise.
- Allah said that Shaytan would have no power over humans except over those who choose to follow him and do wrong.
- Allah told us in the Quran that Shaytan cannot force us to do bad.

Adam's life in the Garden

- Allah created Eve as Adam's wife, and they were asked to live in a garden prepared for them by Allah.
- Allah allowed Adam and Eve to enjoy life in the garden with ONE condition – they could not eat the fruit from one tree in the garden.

- This time, it was the test of Adam and Eve.
- Shaytan enticed them, and they ate the forbidden fruit.
- For this disobedience, Allah ordered Adam, Eve, and Shaytan to leave the Garden.
- Allah ordered Adam and his wife to live on earth for a specific time, and then He will bring them back one day.

Adam and Eve's Repentance

- Adam and Eve realized their mistake and repented (said sorry) immediately for their disobedience.
- Allah forgave both but still wanted them to live on Earth, outside the garden.
- Allah gave them instructions on how to spend time on earth.
- Allah made Adam the first Prophet for humanity at that time.
- Allah said that humans will be tested as Adam and Eve were.
- When He sends guidance to the children of Adam, those who follow will make it to Paradise (Jannah), but those who don't and deny Allah's signs will end up in Hell.

Adam's new role on Earth

- Through these two examples, Allah told us that there will be two tests in this life:
    - Test of arrogance (how do we behave)
    - Test of obedience to Allah
- Adam and Eve brought with them the experience of struggling with Shaytan's tricks in this world. We must learn from them.
- As a Prophet, Adam's role now was to:
    - Make a family of his own and raise children who would live according to Allah's instructions.
    - Spread his generations to populate the Earth.
    - Make a living on earth for himself and his family.
    - Remain on the straight path and continue to guide others on Allah's straight path.
    - Warn people to be aware of the tests Allah gives in this life.

> ### And so began human life on Earth!

Both Adam and Shaytan disobeyed Allah and made a mistake, but there is a difference in their behavior. What is that difference?

Human Qualities come from Allah's Attributes

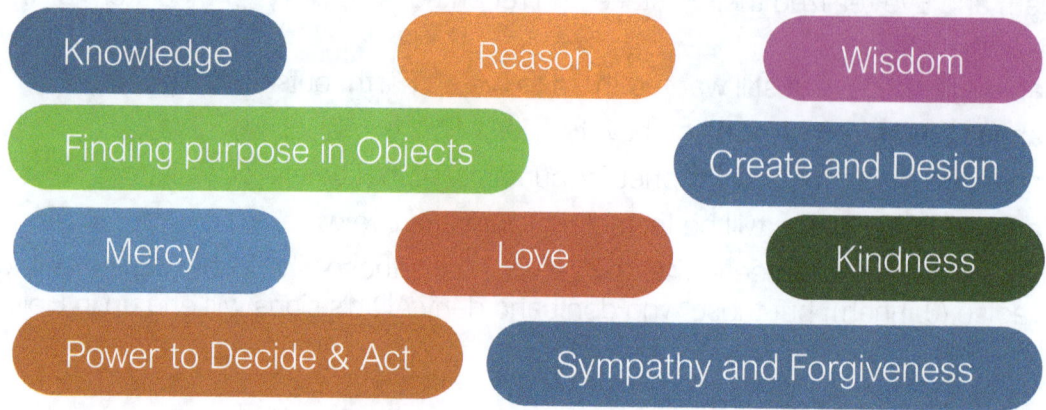

Knowledge   Reason   Wisdom

Finding purpose in Objects   Create and Design

Mercy   Love   Kindness

Power to Decide & Act   Sympathy and Forgiveness

- We got these qualities at the human level because Allah blew something into Adam. However, Allah is perfect in all these qualities.

Lessons Learned

- Making mistakes is OK, but insisting on them and being arrogant about them is unacceptable.
- Both Adam and Shaytan made mistakes, but Shaytan became arrogant, and Adam accepted the mistake.
- Through Adam's story, Allah taught us what challenges we will face in our lives and how we can fail.
- Enjoy this life as long as you are not disobedient to Allah.
- This life is temporary, and ultimately, we will return to Allah.

Be aware of arrogance and disobedience to Allah.

Can you think of other human qualities that are not shown above?

Chapter 7

The Story of Habil (Abel) and Qabil (Cain)

In this chapter, we will learn about one of the earliest evil deeds ever committed on earth.

The Story of Habil and Qabil

- They are the two sons of Adam. In the Islamic traditions, they are called Habil and Qabil. In the Bible, they are called Abel and Cain.

Sacrifices

- It is the story of the first murder on Earth.
- Habil and Qabil wanted to present their sacrifice to Allah (showing their love for Him).
- Habil brought an animal, and Qabil brought his crops.
- Qabil was not righteous and did not fear Allah in his actions.
- Allah accepted Habil's sacrifice but not Qabil's (because of Qabil's bad behavior).
- In those times, people used to get a sign that Allah accepted the sacrifice.
- This made Qabil very angry and jealous.
- Although it is good to compete in good deeds, jealousy is not allowed.

The First Murder

- Qabil realized the issue, but he did not want to accept it.
- Habil told him that Allah only accepts sacrifice from righteous people who fear Allah in their actions. So, be sincere to Allah when presenting the sacrifice.
- Qabil felt angry at Habil and told him he would kill him.
- Because of his good personality, Habil said, even if you try to kill me, I won't try to kill you because I fear Allah, my Creator.
- Qabil murdered him, and that was the first murder ever done in the history of mankind.

The first reaction

- Interestingly, Qabil's first reaction after the murder was that he regretted what he had done

Why did Qabil regret what he had done, because no one had killed before?

The Crow shows Qabil how to bury the dead

- Qabil got worried about what to do with the body of his brother. He did not feel right about leaving it as it is.
- Allah sent down a crow that scratched/dug the ground to hide something.
- Qabil learned how to bury his brother's dead body.
- Since that time, humans have been burying their dead (later, some man-made religions started to burn their dead).

Killing someone is one of the biggest sins

 Allah tells us that murdering someone is as if you murdered all mankind

 Allah tells us that saving someone is like saving all of mankind

 Permanent Hellfire could be the punishment for the murderer on the Day of Judgment

> Which bad attribute in human beings motivated Qabil to do such an evil act, and why should we avoid it?

Lessons Learned

- Jealousy and anger can lead to evil actions that we will regret later in life.
- Habil had the right to defend himself in this case, but he did not. Why do you think he did not?
- When sincere advice is given to us, regardless of who gives it, we should listen and correct our actions.
- Humans can learn from the nature around them.
- Murder is the worst crime one can commit on earth.

Activity

As humans, we have learned a lot from the nature around us. Research an invention that humans have made after learning from the nature around them.

Chapter 8

The Story of Prophet Nuh (AS)

In this chapter, we will learn about the story of Prophet Nuh mentioned in the Quran.

How Mankind became Pagan (Polytheistic)

Generations between Adam and Nuh

- Between Prophet Adam and Prophet Nuh, people still believed in the Oneness of Allah
- Between Adam and Nuh, multiple generations of people had correctly worshipped Allah, following the laws taught by Adam.
- According to the Quran, Nuh lived for more than 950 years!
- Those before Nuh supposedly had an even longer lifespan than he.
- Slowly, the message of Adam disappeared, and innovations appeared.
- In the beginning, the message was clear with no innovations (new things in religion).
- The picture below shows how the message of one God faded over time, while innovations such as worshiping multiple gods grew stronger.

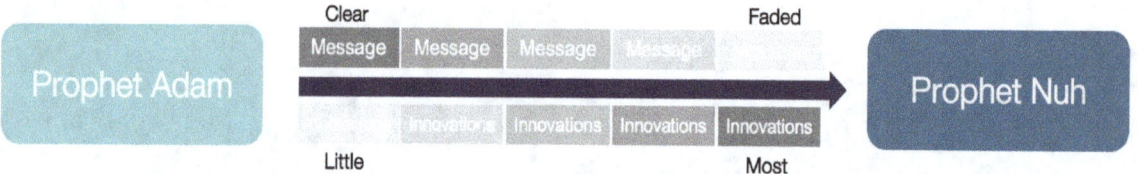

Concept of multiple gods

- By Prophet Nuh's time, people had already forgotten Adam's message. Idol worship took over the message of one Allah.
- After Adam, as time passed, righteous people began to die.
- Good people had started building pictures and statues of their righteous elders for their homes and meeting places.

- These statues were mainly to honor them and, by doing this, to keep their teachings alive.
- People did not worship these statues yet.
- As the people who built these statues died, future generations forgot their purpose and began worshipping them as idols!

In Islam, we are asked to be very careful when drawing pictures or creating statues in honor of people because it may lead to worshiping them.

Nuh's Long Struggle

- Allah sent Prophet Nuh to warn people to stop worshipping idols, or else they would be struck with mishap and disaster.
- Worship is only Allah's right, as He is our Creator and Sustainer.
- Since Nuh was an ordinary farmer, the people of his nation saw nothing special about him or his teachings.

- Since no rich person was following Nuh, they thought the message was unnecessary or even a lie.
- He focused on the leaders of the people first.
- Nuh struggled to teach Allah's message for around a thousand years, but they wouldn't listen.
- He did not lose hope until it became clear to him that they would not pay heed, and that He needed Allah's help.

Leaders Attitude

- As a nation, the people of Nuh were arrogant, especially the rich.
- Their riches made them an arrogant nation.
- Their tribal leaders used to argue with Nuh all the time and even misguide common people through their influence.
- Allah promised them as a nation that if they repented for their behavior, asked for forgiveness, and believed in one God, they would prosper and Allah would bless them.

Arrogance did not allow the people of Nuh to see the Truth, and they rejected him and disobeyed Allah. Does this behavior remind you of anyone in the past before Nuh?

The Result

The Ark and the Flood

- His people's stubbornness (staying in a wrong position) in denying the Oneness of Allah made him sad, and he appealed to Allah (asking Allah for help).
- Allah told Nuh not to be sad or disappointed and to build an ark under His supervision.
- People used to make fun of him because there was no river/sea in the area, and Nuh was making an ark.

- As soon as the ark was built, a great and giant storm began to flood the land.
- Allah told Nuh to take to board the ark, which would sail and cast anchor:
    - A few animal pairs (most probably cattle) that is needed to survive in the new place.
    - Members of his family and other people who believed in the oneness of Allah.

The Fate of the Ark

- Nuh's son, a disbeliever, refused to join him and drowned. The waves were very high, and Prophet Nuh told his son to be safe on the boat.
- He said no, I would be safe on a mountain. But no one was safe that day except those who obeyed Allah.
- The Storm eventually stopped, and the waves did, too. Allah ordered the earth to swallow all the water.
- The Ark came to rest on Mount Judi.
- Nuh was sad about his son's drowning and appealed to Allah. Allah declared that since Nuh's son was evil, he was not part of his family.
- Prophet Nuh and everyone aboard got down from the Ark in peace and with Allah's blessings for those who had come with him.

A couple of misconceptions

✕ The flood covered the entire Earth.
✕ Nuh took animals from every species with him.

- Since the punishment was given to the people of Nuh, the flood with heavy winds came only in the area where they lived. There is no reason to punish everyone living on Earth at that time because not everyone got the message of Prophet Nuh. It is God's practice that when a nation rejects a Messenger, it is punished on Earth before the Day of Judgment.

- Also, since Prophet Nuh was supposed to land on a distant land after the flood, God asked him to take pairs of animals that humans usually use for food or transportation. This way, he and the survivors could start their lives immediately in a remote land that is their new home.

Lessons Learned

- There is no sound reason to worship anyone except Allah.
- People often worship idols because they have seen their parents doing it. Often, they don't have a reason for doing so.
- Even though idols started as mere ways to celebrate people, they quickly became objects of worship.
- We can praise people and appreciate them, but we should never begin to 'worship' them by blindly following them in everything.
- Relationships won't matter in the eyes of Allah when it comes to following the commands of Allah; what matters is your actions.
- Give everyone the rights that they deserve, nothing more, nothing less.

Do you see any reasons for people to worship anyone or anything other than Allah or multiple gods?

Activity

Hand-draw a picture of a giant ark with humans and animals from your imagination. Show it to everyone in the next class.

Chapter 9

The Story of Aad and Thamud

In this chapter, we will learn about the two giant nations of Aad and Thamud, whom Allah destroyed because of their arrogance.

What is a Miracle?

- Many prophets and messengers were given miracles to meet the challenges they faced. A miracle is something very special that happens and cannot be explained by ordinary reasons.
- It is not possible to confirm that every Prophet was given a miracle. The miracles of some of those prophets are mentioned in the Quran.
- The miracles are given for three reasons:
    - To protect the Prophet from the injustices committed by his people when they oppose him.
    - To show the people around him that Allah is with the Prophet.
    - To increase the faith of the believers in the Prophet, so that they are sure that they are on the right side.
- All miracles happen with Allah's permission. No Prophet or Messenger can do it on their own.
- Some of the examples of the miracles given to the Prophets are:
    - Prophet Musa could turn his staff (stick) into a giant snake because people in his time were magicians, and it allowed him to fight back.
    - Prophet Isa (Jesus) could heal the sick or bring the dead to life with the permission of Allah.
- The physical miracle is only visible to people who can see it at that time.
- Prophet Muhammad was given a very different miracle. He was given the Quran as a living miracle, a book that is miraculous not only for those who received it but for everyone until the Day of Judgment.

Allah has sent Prophets to Every Nation

- Remember, Allah made the promise about guidance when He asked Adam and Eve to start their lives in this world? Allah fulfilled His promise.
- Prophet Muhammad told us, through the Quran and many narrations, that Allah sent many Prophets and Messengers. Every major nation at the center of a civilization received a Prophet or Messenger.
- Which means that Allah, through His prophets and messengers, has sent guidance and his teachings directly or indirectly to **every nation** on this Earth.
- For example, Prophet Muhammad came to Makkah and settled in Medina, but then, through the Caliphate and the companions of the Prophet, the rest of the world came to know about him and the guidance of Allah.
- And the message is simple: there is only one God, Allah, who should be worshiped alone; do good deeds; and one day He will hold everyone accountable (asked about) for their deeds done in this world.
- All the other information that we learn in Islam is the details of this simple message.
- The nations of Aad and Thamud were once big and powerful, and Allah sent messengers to them with guidance already rooted in their nature, but they forgot it and began acting arrogantly towards others.
- Let's learn about them.

Prophet Hud (AS)

The people of Aad

- The people of Aad ruled a grand city called *Iram*, an important stop on a trade route.
- It is said they were also physically well-built and strong.
- Their city had tall buildings and guard towers. This was unique at the time.
- Their rulers were arrogant and treated their people with great injustice.

- They mistreated the people of local villages and tribes by charging them high tax rates.
- They were polytheists (worshiping man-made gods) – not believing in one True God.
- They made travelers through their town pay tribute to their idols to get money from them.

Allah chose Prophet Hud

- As promised to Adam, Allah also wanted to guide and discipline the People of Aad. He picked a young gentleman named Hud for this job.
- Allah chooses a Prophet or a Messenger among a people. The Quran does not say how He chooses that person.

- He was not wealthy, but was considered trustworthy by the common people.
- Hud received revelations (messages from God) from Allah about his prophethood and his responsibilities as a Prophet.
- As did Prophet Nuh, Prophet Hud reached out to the leaders of the nation and told them that he was a Messenger of God, sent with a true message grounded in high morals that would allow his nation to not only prosper in this world but also in the next.
- The Quran does not mention what miracle was given to Prophet Hud.

Their objections

- When Prophet Hud started giving them the message, they raised a few objections:

1	2	3
Worship Allah Alone	**Human Prophet**	**Life After Death**
"Our forefathers have been worshiping idols for centuries. How can Hud be right, even if it makes sense?"	Hud is just a human. If he is a messenger of Allah, he must be some supernatural (not from the natural world) being, like an angel	Hud says that after we all die and turn into dust and bones, Allah will bring us to life again for another world. How is it even possible?

His Appeal to Aad

- Prophet Hud sincerely advised them on all three points raised and tried to answer every question they had – he treated them like his brothers. He told them:
  - They should worship the Creator who created them, not what the forefathers used to worship. These idols are hand-made, so they cannot be God.
  - It makes sense to send a human being as a Prophet among human beings; otherwise, how would he become a role model for them?
  - If there is no Hereafter, then how will bad people be punished for their evil deeds and good people be rewarded for their good deeds?
- At the same time, he warned them to recognize the oneness of Allah and to understand that they had no other gods but Him.
- He urged them to seek Allah's forgiveness and not use their power with force on the poor people.
- His nation considered him a liar and repeatedly demanded more proof that his teachings were true.
- They would not try to discuss and understand.
- They said they would not leave their idols because their fathers had worshiped them, and their powers came from them.
- However, very few young people believed in him and followed his teachings.

The Punishment

- The nation was struck by drought for an unusually long period.
- After warning them for some time, Allah told Prophet Hud to gather his followers and leave the city immediately.

- The people of the town saw a few large clouds approaching. They got overjoyed because they thought these were the rain clouds they were waiting for.
- The people of Aad were struck by a windstorm caused by clouds that tore caravans and people out of their path.
- The windstorm raged for seven days and eight nights.
- The city of Aad was lost forever and is now remembered only in legends.

فَلَمَّا رَأَوْهُ عَارِضًا مُّسْتَقْبِلَ أَوْدِيَتِهِمْ ۙ قَالُوا هٰذَا عَارِضٌ مُّمْطِرُنَا ۚ بَلْ هُوَ مَا اسْتَعْجَلْتُم بِهِ ۖ رِيحٌ فِيهَا عَذَابٌ أَلِيمٌ

تُدَمِّرُ كُلَّ شَىْءٍ بِأَمْرِ رَبِّهَا فَأَصْبَحُوا لَا يُرَىٰ إِلَّا مَسَاكِنُهُمْ ۚ كَذٰلِكَ نَجْزِى الْقَوْمَ الْمُجْرِمِينَ

Then, when they saw [with which they had been threatened] that a cloud was speedily advancing towards their valleys, they said: "This is a cloud which will rain for us." (Hud told them) No! In fact, this is the same thing you sought to hasten: a furious wind containing a woeful affliction. It will destroy everything at the behest of its Lord. Then, they became such that nothing could be seen there except their broken houses. That's how We punish the criminals (46:24-25)

وَ أَمَّا عَادٌ فَأُهْلِكُوا بِرِيحٍ صَرْصَرٍ عَاتِيَةٍ

سَخَّرَهَا عَلَيْهِمْ سَبْعَ لَيَالٍ وَّ ثَمٰنِيَةَ أَيَّامٍ ۙ حُسُومًا ۖ فَتَرَى الْقَوْمَ فِيهَا صَرْعَىٰ ۚ كَأَنَّهُمْ أَعْجَازُ نَخْلٍ خَاوِيَةٍ

فَهَلْ تَرَىٰ لَهُم مِّنْ بَاقِيَةٍ

And (We destroyed) Aad by a stormy windstorm, fierce and unrestrained. God let this windstorm on them for seven nights and eight days ravage them. Then you would have seen those people lying overthrown as though they were hollow trunks of palm trees. So, do you now see any of them remaining? (69:4-8)

Two important points

Why did Allah punish nations?

- When Allah sends His Messengers (Rasool) to a nation and the Messenger provides proof about one True God, the Day of Judgment, and that he is sent from that God, they are required to accept this message because it is the truth.

- The nation as a whole may or may not accept the message and change its behavior. However, the Messengers warn them of a punishment directly from Allah if they don't accept the message.

- However, those who accepted the message received the good news that they would be saved.

- Allah punishes the nation for the following reasons:
  - To prove the point to the nation that the message and messenger are from Allah, and they don't have an option to reject it.
  - The nation is punished and recorded in history so that nations coming after it can learn from it. Their fate (results) proves to other nations that Allah controls this world, and their actions will be judged one day.

Natural disasters

- The majority of these nations were punished by angels through natural disasters. The details of those are mentioned in the Quran.

- However, it must be kept in mind that the natural disasters that we face today are not a punishment from God.

- The punishment through natural disaster only comes when God's messenger is present among the nation.

- The natural disasters we face today are mostly tests from Allah, so He can test us on how patient we are in such situations and how we help those affected by the disaster.

Prophet Saleh (AS)

The People of Thamud

- The people of Thamud lived about 3,000 years ago and succeeded the people of Aad. They controlled a fertile (ideal for vegetation) patch of land that surrounded many natural resources.
- They built many castles and maintained an army of soldiers to protect their wealth and power.
- If they did allow some to bring their herds to benefit from these natural resources, they charged huge fees.
- They built their cities and castles right out of the mountain, and they were considered experts in it.
- The rich people were benefiting from the resources.
- They worshipped Allah, but also other idols like Aad.
- Their excuses were very similar to Aad's about idols and life after death.

Allah chose Saleh

- Allah chose a young man named Saleh from the ruling tribe to be the prophet of this nation.
- Prophet Saleh worked hard to convince his people to change their ways by letting common people use their wells and other natural resources.
- He also taught them to worship only Allah, give up the worship of idols, and ask Allah for forgiveness.
- He also told them about his prophethood and the accountability they would face on the Day of Judgment.
- They also knew about the people of Aad and their fate.
- They blamed him for being a magician because a few young people supported him.
- The people of Thamud asked him to bring a sign (miracle) to prove his truthfulness – but in their hearts, they were not serious about the message.

Miracle became a test

- Prophet Saleh warned them that Allah would show them the sign, but the results of denying it would be severe.
- Allah made a camel appear from the mountains (a miracle).
- Prophet Saleh told his people that Allah's she-camel would have her turn to drink from the water resource, and they would have their turn to let their animals drink from the resource.

- He asked his people not to harm the she-camel, or Allah would punish them. This became a test for them because they were not very generous in sharing their natural resources with others.
- When people ask Allah for a sign through their prophets, and if Allah gives them the sign, then denying the sign becomes a serious disobedience, and the people are punished by Allah.

Killing the camel and punishment

- The people of Thamud knew that this was a camel from Allah because of its miraculous nature (naturally impossible).
- Prophet Saleh also repeatedly warned them not to harm the camel, as it was a sign.

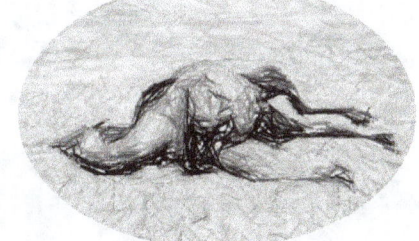

- Some wicked people among the Thamud killed the camel out of arrogance. It was expected that the leaders of Thamud would stop this killing, but it did not happen, and they simply were observers.
- Allah asked Prophet Saleh to take the believers and leave the town. Give them three days, and severe punishment will come.
- Allah punished them with a single blast on the ground that destroyed them (a type of earthquake with a loud sound).
- It is also said that multiple severe earthquakes destroyed them at once.
- All the believers with Prophet Saleh were saved from this horrible event.

What should our role be when a wrong is happening in a society that affects the entire society?

Lessons Learned

- What is given by Allah on this earth is a shared blessing from Him – no one nation should control it, but rather share it with other nations.
- Too much wealth and blessings sometimes make people arrogant – be careful about it.
- Rulers/Leaders in a nation are important people – they decide a nation's future.
- We have a lesson in these stories: like these nations, we will be held responsible for our actions in this world; we will be held responsible on the Day of Judgment.
- Corrupt nations face consequences in this world, one way or another.
- Allah has destroyed very strong nations before due to their arrogance and injustices.

Chapter 10

The Story of Ibrahim (AS)

In this chapter, we will learn about a great Prophet, Prophet Ibrahim (AS), who is considered the father of so many Prophets who came to the Children of Israel and Ismail.

Father of a generation of Prophets

All Prophets after Ibrahim came from his two sons, Ismail and Ishaq. Allah honored Prophet Ibrahim due to his obedience to Him.

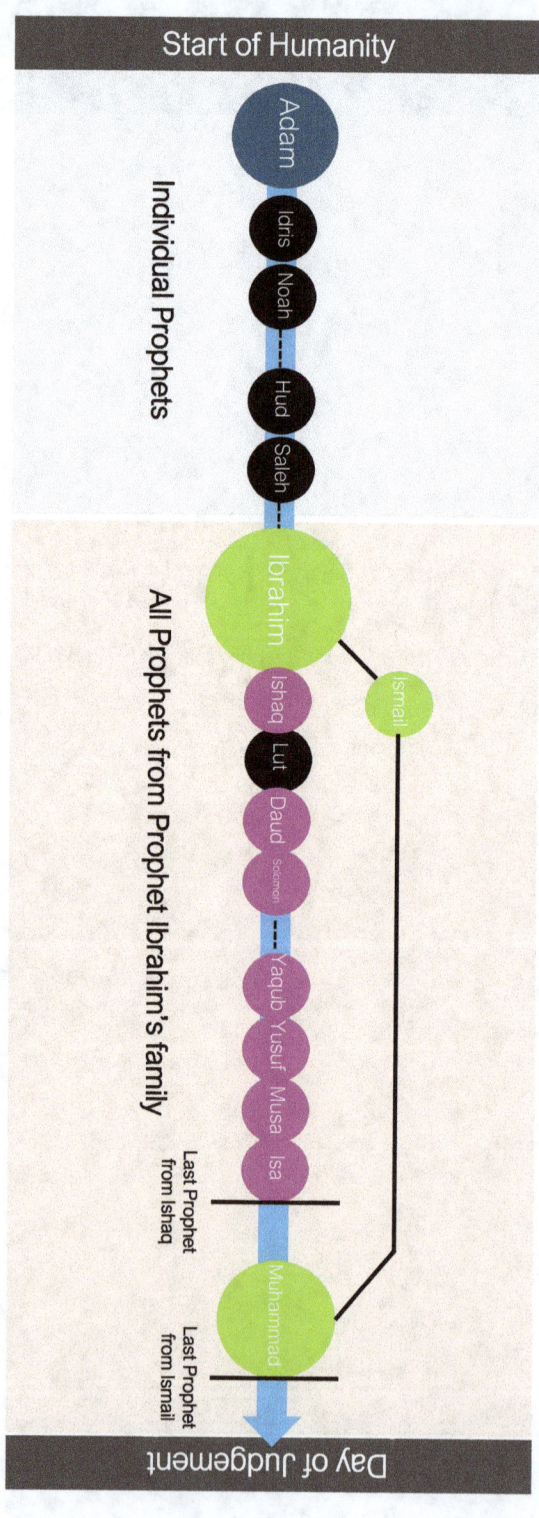

Prophet Ibrahim (AS)

The status of Prophet Ibrahim

- Prophet Ibrahim is called the Father of the Prophets. Many prophets and nations are from his children, including the nations of Musa, Jesus, Ishaq, Ismail, Yaqoob, Yusuf, Dawood, Suleiman, and Muhammad (Peace be upon all of them)
- It is an honor given to him for his devotion (focus) to Allah and His commands. He went through many tests and trials, and he passed them all with flying colors.
- Judaism, Christianity, and Islam are collectively known as the Abrahamic religions because they all acknowledge Abraham as a main figure in their faith traditions, despite differences in their understanding of his teachings.
- Although the true teachings of Prophet Ibrahim are only present in Islam. All other nations have changed his teachings.
- Because of his devotion to Allah, Allah called him His friend (Khaleel ullah), which is a great honor.

His family

- He was born in Mesopotamia—current-day Iraq—around 1900 BCE.
- At that time, people worshipped statues. They were polytheistic and also worshiped natural objects, such as the sun and moon.
- His father, at that time, was a sculptor who made statues that people bought as idols to worship.
- When he became a prophet and started receiving revelations from Allah, he began to write them on leather scrolls (sheets).

Conflict with his father

- Once he received prophethood and was introduced to Allah, Ibrahim invited his father to believe in Allah, who made the entire world.
- His father and the family were engaged in making idols and selling them.
- Ibrahim's father rejected what Ibrahim had to say, got angry, and threatened to stone his son to death.
- The father also told his son Ibrahim to leave his house.
- The family did not want to go against the tradition (practice) of their elders.
- Despite this behavior, Prophet Ibrahim remained very gentle with his father and promised to make dua to Allah for him.

His Search for God

- Ibrahim was a curious child who wanted to learn what was right and wrong.
- Idol worship made no sense to Ibrahim, so he began seeking the truth about who created this world and who the Creator is.
- Every human being asks this question: Who created me, and who is that Creator?

Wise Teaching

- To expose the weaknesses in their beliefs, he highlighted a few key points.
- First, he looked at the stars and called them gods, but in the morning they disappeared.
- Then he looked at the Moon and called it a god, but it disappeared in the morning as well.

- Then he looked at the sun, the brightest object he could see, and called it god, but then it disappeared at night.
- He concluded that showing them the fact that these objects could not be God, so why were they making idols of such objects, including humans?
- These objects are following a specific routine and have no mind of their own. They cannot be God.

What should our behavior be toward our parents, even if we do not like something or disagree with them?

Wisdom in giving the message of God

- Ibrahim began calling people to worship One God.

- His people did not listen because they were accustomed to worshipping idols that were supposed to fulfill their wishes.

- One day, when the temple with the most important idols was left unguarded, Ibrahim entered it.

The big guy

- He smashed the idols and threw them on the ground. But he left one big idol standing.

- The priests returned and found out that it was possibly Ibrahim who had done this. The priests asked Ibrahim if he had destroyed their idols.

- He told the priests to ask the biggest idol, and it could tell them what happened.

- The priests knew that these idols couldn't speak. They first seemed uncomfortable, but then said, "You know they cannot speak".

- He told them that if the idols could not speak and could not benefit or harm them, then they were not worthy of being worshipped.

- They got angry hearing that took him to the King, who used to call himself god-king, and they had an argument:

  - **King:** O Ibrahim, tell me who is your Lord?
  - **Ibrahim:** He is the one who gives life and takes it away.
  - **King:** I also give life and death by my command.
  - **Ibrahim:** My Lord raises the sun from the East. Bring it from the West, if you can.

- The King did not know what to say and got angry with Ibrahim.

- The priests and leaders told the King that Ibrahim had tried to lead people away from idol worship.

- The King ordered Ibrahim to be thrown into the fire.

- The evil people threw Ibrahim into the fire, but Allah had other plans for Ibrahim.

- Allah ordered the fire to cool down and become a safe place for Ibrahim.

- Allah then commanded Ibrahim to leave Mesopotamia and settle elsewhere.

We ordered, "O fire, be cool and safety upon Ibrahim." (21:69)

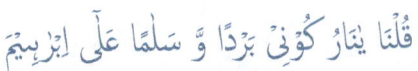

Two giant nations are born

Makkah – Children of Ismail

Their center is Makkah
People from the Arab world

Palestine – Children of Israel

Their center is Palestine
Mostly Jews

- In his new home of Palestine, Ibrahim married Sarah, but they had no children.
- He then married Hajrah, with whom he had a son named Ismail.
- Later, Ibrahim and Sarah also had a son named Ishaq.
- Allah gave him children when he and his wife were very old and had no expectations of having children. Allah did that to make His plans work for Ibrahim.
- Allah had ordered him to settle Hajrah and her son Ismail in the land of Makkah.
- Later, Ismail would fulfill the role of a prophet in this land.
- Sarah and her son, Ishaq, remained in Palestine. Ishaq would also play the role of a prophet in Palestine.
- Both children of Prophet Ibrahim laid the foundation for two major nations: the Children of Israel and the Children of Ismail.
- That's why Prophet Ibrahim is called the Father of these two big nations, and three major religions, Judaism, Christianity, and Islam associate themselves with Prophet Ibrahim. These are called the Abrahamic Religions.

Lessons Learned

- When we believe and follow something, it must be right and ethical. Just because our elders do something is not a good reason.
- Allah has put many lessons for us to learn from the universe around us.
- It is a perfect design that has everything we need – a wise God must have created it.
- The Messengers of Allah are directly under the protection of Allah, and He does not allow wicked people to harm them because he is presenting the message of Allah to people on His behalf.
- Ibrahim trusted Allah, and Allah saved him from the fire.
- Prophet Ibrahim went through many tests, and he passed them all with flying colors.
- We must use wisdom when sharing our faith with others.

Chapter 11

The Story of Ismail (AS)

In this chapter, we will learn about Prophet Ismail, who founded a great nation in the lands of Arabia, which later laid the foundation of today's Muslim world.

Prophet Ismail (AS)

The dream of Prophet Ibrahim

- Prophet Ismail, the first son of Prophet Ibrahim, was born to his second wife, Haajra.
- Allah gave Prophet Ibrahim a child in his old age, when he was not expecting one. He had been making dua for one.
- Allah planned to make Prophet Ismail the father of a great nation centered in Makkah.
- When Prophet Ismail was a young boy (around 13-14 years), Prophet Ibrahim had a dream in which Allah ordered him to "sacrifice" his son.

Kabaah was originally built thousands of years ago!

- What Allah meant by "sacrifice" was that Allah wanted to ask Ibrahim to dedicate his son to the upkeep of Kabaah, His house of worship.
- Ibrahim misunderstood and left for Mina with Ismail, the place he had seen in his dream.
- Prophet Ibrahim told Ismail about his dream.

The Response of Prophet Ismail

- Being the son of Prophet Ibrahim, Prophet Ismail told him he was not afraid of being "sacrificed (killed)" by Allah's orders.
- He told Prophet Ibrahim to do as Allah said.
- Prophet Ismail, very calmly, lay down on the ground and closed his eyes.
- Prophet Ibrahim picked up his knife for the "sacrifice".
- But the angel Jibrael appeared with a ram (male sheep) to be sacrificed in its place.
- Prophet Ismail was saved!
- As a reward, Allah commanded Muslims to observe this day as Eid al-Adha or the "Feast of Sacrifice".
- Prophet Ibrahim was a true believer and a 'Muslim'. He passed Allah's many difficult tests like these.

Obey Allah

Reward from Allah

The dreams of prophets are unlike those of regular people. The events/facts that the prophets see in their dreams are either true dreams (that will come true in the future) or very important news symbolically conveyed to them (for example, mosques symbolize prayers). These dreams only appear to them when they are made prophets. For example, in this dream, the sacrifice means to dedicate the child to a purpose. When Prophet Ismail is dedicated to the Kabaah, it will be a sacrifice from Prophet Ibrahim because now he cannot ask him to do anything else.

Building the Kaaba

- Prophet Ibrahim was ordered by Allah to build the Kaaba (for which Ismail was to be dedicated). He asked his son, Ismail, for help, and they both built the foundation and the building.

- Ibrahim and Ismail laid the foundation of the House of Allah. Ismail brought stones from the hills surrounding the Kaaba, while Ibrahim built.

- When the walls became high, Ismail brought a stone for Ibrahim to stand on so he could continue building.

- They both prayed to Allah to accept their service and also made a dua for a Prophet and a nation that will reside here and accept it.

وَ اِذْ يَرْفَعُ اِبْرٰهٖمُ الْقَوَاعِدَ مِنَ الْبَيْتِ وَ اِسْمٰعِيْلُ ۚ رَبَّنَا تَقَبَّلْ مِنَّا ۚ اِنَّكَ اَنْتَ السَّمِيْعُ الْعَلِيْمُ

And recall when Ibrahim and Ismail were raising the foundations of this House, saying, "O Lord! Accept our prayer (and efforts) from us. Undoubtedly, it is only You who hears all and knows all." (2:127)

Have you ever seen an animal sacrifice on Eid al-Adha? Share your experience with others.

Children of Ismail and their responsibility

Allah created a huge nation from the Children of Ismail	Today's Arab world, especially people around Saudi Arabia, are from the Children of Ismail.
They were mostly idol worshippers before the time of Prophet Muhammad	Prophet Muhammad was sent to them as the last prophet on earth. They were made the protectors of the Quran after Prophet Muhammad left this world.

The role of the Children of Ismail

- Prophet Muhammad told us there will be no Prophet after him, and the Quran is the only main source of guidance for humanity now.
- However, the Quran will not reach other nations on its own.

- The Children of Ismail, specifically, Muslims, in general, are given the responsibility by Allah to give the Quran and the message of Allah to other nations in the world.
- They are the flag bearers of Islam now. The Quran described their role as the middle nation. If someone wants to learn about Islam and the Quran, they will come to Muslims.

- Allah has made the Children of Ismail the "Middle Nation." Middle means to come between two things
- Prophet Muhammad gave the Quran and Sunnah to the Children of Ismail (Arabs of that time), and their responsibility was/is to deliver it to the rest of the world
- The Children of Ismail must present the truth of Islam to the rest of the world now.
- The non-Arab Muslims are part of that middle nation now because we have become Muslims, and we should help them with this difficult task.

Custodian of the Kaaba

- Prophet Ibrahim had prayed that Allah would keep his family the custodians (caretakers) of the Kabaah.
- For thousands of years, the guardianship (caretakers) of the Kabaah remained in the family of Ismail.
- Although there were a few changes in history, the guardianship again came to the family of the Prophet Muhammad, who was from the Children of Ismail, the last prophet on earth.

Lessons Learned

- The Quran calls Prophet Ibrahim the friend of Allah because he obeyed Allah in everything he was asked.
- If a person has strong faith, they will follow Allah's commands without asking questions.
- Allah rewards people who are ready to follow His commands in this world and the Hereafter.
- If we have strong faith, then Allah will test us often.
- When we are tested, keep an eye on the reward, not on the problem we are going through.
- People of the world will learn about Islam through us.

Chapter 12

The Story of Kabaah

In this chapter, we will learn about the Kabaah, the center of worship for all Muslims, which we call the House of Allah.

History of Kabaah

When was the Kabaah first built?

- Before Prophet Ibrahim's family arrived, Makkah was uninhabited (no people lived there).
- Some 4,000 years ago (2000 BC), Allah ordered Prophet Ibrahim to build the Kabaah.
- First, he could not find a trace of the Kabaah – it had disappeared due to floods and the passage of time.

- With the help of Allah, he discovered the original foundation built by Prophet Adam.
- Ibrahim, with the help of his son Ismail, constructed a roofless building by using rocks from around the surrounding hills.
- Many people and tribes became the caretakers of Kabaah after Prophet Ibrahim and Ismail built it, but almost a century before the birth of the Prophet Muhammad, the Children of Ismail again became the custodians (caretakers) of the Kabaah.

Kabaah in Different Times in History

The Construction of Kabaah

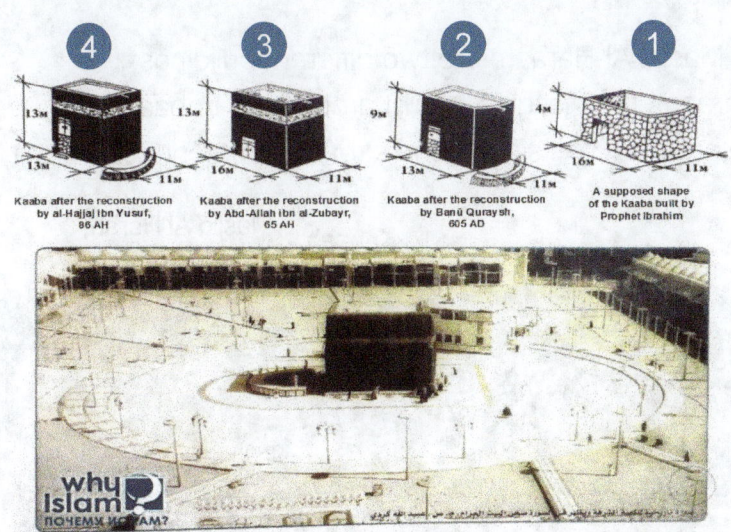

- The original construction did not stay intact and was destroyed over time.
- The Kabaah was destroyed or damaged on multiple occasions and rebuilt several times.
- During various reconstructions, Hateem was included inside the Kabaah. Originally, it was part of the Kabaah, which Quraysh could not cover due to a shortage of funds.

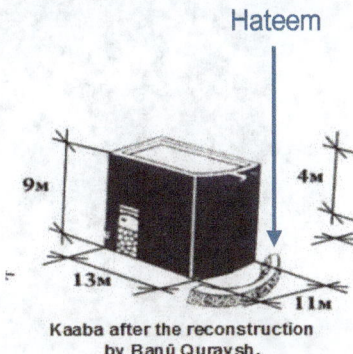

Hateem

Kaaba after the reconstruction
by Banû Quraysh,
605 AD

- Before prophethood, Prophet Muhammad also participated in the reconstruction of Kabaah.
- When it was time to replace the black stone, a dispute emerged – every tribe wanted to have the honor.
- Prophet Muhammad got the opportunity to replace it.

- Prophet Muhammad laid a sheet on the ground and placed the black stone at its center. He then asked the leaders to lift the blanket from its sides and climb the wall himself. When the blanket was raised, he took the stone and put it in its place himself. He used his God-given wisdom to solve this big issue.
- Black Stone is situated in the southeastern corner of Kabaah, which is used to begin the Tawaf after kissing/touching it, or by waving the hands toward it. It is like making a promise to Allah before beginning the tawaf.

Importance of Kabaah and Masjid Al-Haraam

Masjid Al-Haraam

- Kabaah and Masjid Al-Haraam are two different buildings.
- Masjid Al-Haraam, the mosque, is built around the Kabaah.
- The mosque around it has since been expanded and now covers a large area.

Kabaah   Masjid Al Haram

Masjid Al Haram is built around the Kabaah

Qibla (direction for prayers)

- **Qibla:** the direction that Muslims face during prayer.
- Kabaah is important for three reasons: It is the center of worshiping Allah alone, it is the Qibla for Muslims for praying, and it is also the place for Hajj.
- For the Children of Israel, once Bayt al Maqdis (Masjid Al-Aqsa in Palestine) was constructed, it was then considered the Qibla for them.
- However, Kabaah in Makkah has always been the Qibla for the Children of Ismail since it was built by Prophet Ibrahim.

Situation of Qibla in the time of Prophet Muhammad

- In the beginning, Prophet Muhammad was directed by Allah to face Bayt al-Maqdis (Jerusalem) for prayer.
- The reason was to test the Children of Ismail (his companions, to be specific) – to see if they would follow the Prophet or disobey him because of their bias and attachment toward the Kabaah.
- Later, Allah changed the Qibla back towards Masjid al-Haram or the Kabaah because Prophet Muhammad also wanted the same.

- This change in the Qibla became a test for the Children of Israel in Medinah (Jews, specifically).
- God tested both nations through this change of Qibla.

Importance in today's world

- It is a symbolic House of Allah, dedicated to His worship – He does not live there.
- Prophet Ibrahim built the Kabaah for all of humanity to worship the One True God.

- A place of security for all humans – that's why it is called Masjid Al Haram, because fighting/war is not allowed in this area.
- If someone takes shelter in the Kabaah, he is guaranteed safety and security (unless Allah commands otherwise).
- It offers a sense of unity among all Muslims worldwide.

Tawaf of Kabaah

Tawaf never stood

- The ritual of circling the Kabaah is performed seven times to complete the worship.
- When one visits the Kabaah, one must perform the Tawaf of the Kabaah as the first thing.
- Prophet Muhammad called this practice "Saying greetings to Kabaah" (like in a mosque, we pray 2 rakah).

- It symbolizes the unity of the believers in the worship of One God.
- Everything revolves around Allah, and humans should live their lives thinking about, remembering, and obeying Allah. In Tawaf, we do the same.

Hajj and Umrah

- Hajj is a ritual (worship) that every sane and adult Muslim must perform once in their lifetime.
- Hajj is a symbolic war against Satan. The war that humans must fight against Satan throughout their lives has been symbolized in the Hajj.
- We dedicate our lives and devote our wealth to this war.

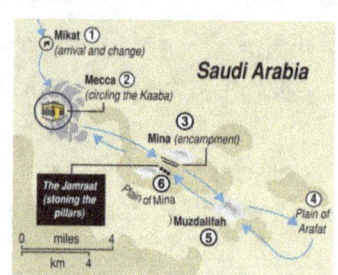

- The steps involved in Hajj are shown below:

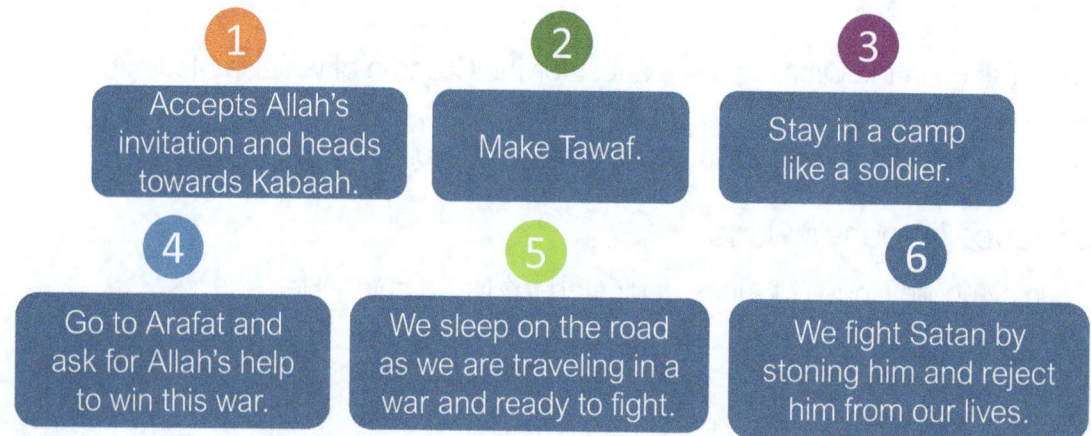

1 Accepts Allah's invitation and heads towards Kabaah.

2 Make Tawaf.

3 Stay in a camp like a soldier.

4 Go to Arafat and ask for Allah's help to win this war.

5 We sleep on the road as we are traveling in a war and ready to fight.

6 We fight Satan by stoning him and reject him from our lives.

Umrah

- It is a minor Hajj if we cannot afford the actual Hajj for any valid reason.
- Acknowledgment (recognizing) of the blessings of Allah.
- Affirmation (acceptance) of Allah's Tawhid (Oneness of God).
- This is a reminder that, after embracing (accepting) Islam, we have devoted ourselves to Him.
- Through Umrah, we renew that commitment (dedication) to Allah.

If any of you have visited Makkah for Umrah, please share your experience with the class.

Lessons Learned

- Allah has dedicated a place on earth that reminds us and unites us on the ONENESS OF ALLAH.
- Praying towards the Kabaah from anywhere in the world teaches us a sense of discipline.
- The story of replacing the black stone teaches us how to include everyone in good acts.
- Use wisdom when dealing with conflicts between people.
- In this life, there is a constant fight with Shaytan, and we must be prepared to fight back and win it.
- We must honor and respect the places and symbols, especially those that are related to Allah.

Chapter 13

The Story of Yusuf (AS)

In this chapter, we will learn about one of the Quran's unique stories, that of Prophet Yusuf (AS). This entire story is contained in one Surah.

The Family of Yusuf (AS)

- Prophet Yusuf is from the family of Prophet Ibrahim on the side of Prophet Ishaq, who was the younger son of Prophet Ibrahim.

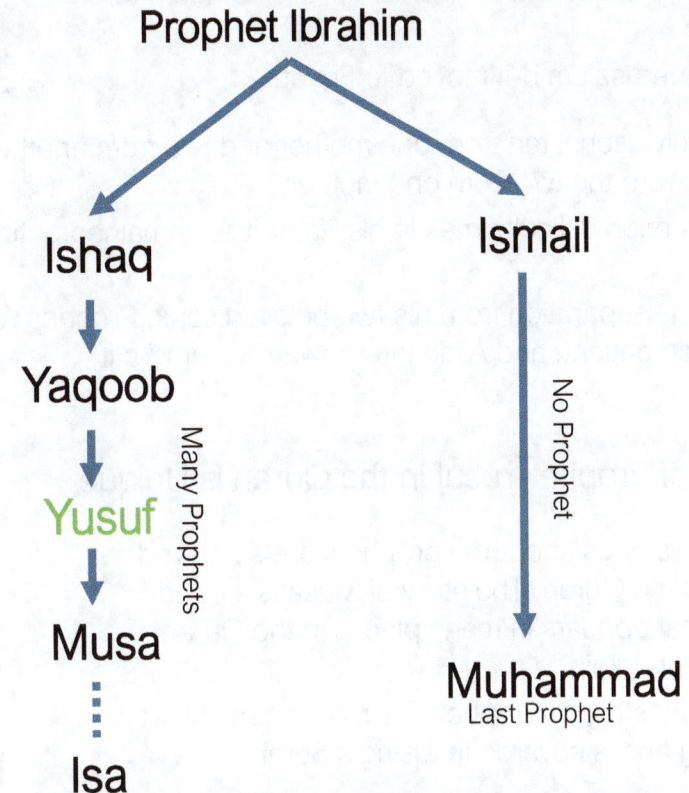

Prophet Ibrahim

Ishaq → Yaqoob → Yusuf → Musa ⋮ Isa

Many Prophets

Ismail

No Prophet

Muhammad
Last Prophet

Prophet Ishaq

- He was the younger son of Prophet Ibrahim and his wife, Sarah, and settled in Palestine.
- He was the forefather of a generation of prophets.
- His birth was predicted by angels and mentioned in the Quran.
- He was Allah's gift to Prophet Ibrahim in his old age.
- His generation was called Bani Israel (his son Yaqoob's other name was Israel).

Prophet Yaqoob

- He was the son of Prophet Ishaq, father of Prophet Yusuf.
- Also known as "Israel," which means "Servant of Allah". "Bani Israel," or the Children of Israel, are named after him.
- He lived in Jerusalem but moved to Egypt.

- He had twelve sons, ten from one mother and two from another. Prophet Yusuf and Bin Yamin were the two from one mother.
- He went through difficult times in his life, but he remained patient and never lost hope in Allah.
- He faced the separation from his two beloved sons, Prophet Yusuf and Bin Yamin, but he remained patient, and Allah later rewarded him for it.

The story of Prophet Yusuf in the Quran is Unique

- Most of the stories about the prophets are scattered throughout the Quran. The story of Musa is a good example that appears in many places in the Quran with different details.

- However, the story of Prophet Yusuf is unique in that it is very long and is covered in a single Surah.

- The Quran called it the "best of the stories" and suggests that it teaches many lessons for Muslims across time and place.
- Jews and Christians of the time of the Prophet Muhammad could also relate to this story, as it is mentioned in the Bible in great detail.
- The children of Prophet Yusuf and his eleven brothers formed the eleven tribes in Egypt, whose later generations were enslaved by the Pharaoh.
- Prophet Musa got them freed with the help of Allah.
- We will learn more about Prophet Musa in the later chapters.

The Story of Prophet Yusuf

Prophet Yusuf and his brothers

- Prophet Yusuf was among the 12 sons of Prophet Yaqoob.
- Being a prophet of Allah, Prophet Yaqoob knew that there was something special about Yusuf, as he was a very wise, kind, and loving boy.
- The ten step-brothers of Yusuf were very jealous of him and his real brother, Bin-Yamin (Benjamin). They thought their father loved Prophet Yusuf more than he loved them.

His dream

- One day, Prophet Yusuf told his father he had a strange (weird) dream. He saw eleven stars, the sun, and the moon, all bowing to him.
- In Islam, we are not allowed to bow down to anyone except Allah, so it was a very strange dream that Prophet Yusuf could not understand.
- Prophet Yaqoob told him not to tell any of his brothers about the dream because they would become jealous.
- He knew there was something behind this dream that he could not understand then, but soon everyone would see it come true.

Gift of interpreting dreams

- Prophet Yaqoob knew that Allah had chosen him and would teach him how to interpret dreams.
- Later, Prophet Yusuf would interpret other people's dreams, including a king's dream.
- However, he realized the truth behind his dream only after he saw it with his own eyes.
- Interestingly, he was able to interpret other people's dreams but not his.

Share any of your good dreams with the class. It is recommended by scholars of Islam not to share bad dreams.

The Plot to Kill Yusuf

- They wanted their father's attention and love while acting mischievously all the time. They became jealous, as the Prophet Yaqub had expected.
- Prophet Yaqub loved Prophet Yusuf so much that he would not allow his brothers to take him anywhere with them, fearing that some animal might eat him, as this was very common at the time.

- However, jealousy does not let anyone sit peacefully. One of the brothers suggested killing Yusuf or sending him away to some far-off land.
- They decided to throw him down a well.
- They asked their father's permission to take Yusuf out for a day of fun.
- Their father did not agree at first, but finally allowed it after they promised to keep him safe.
- The brothers threw Yusuf into a dark, dried-up well.

"A wolf ate Yusuf"

- Allah comforted Yusuf by inspiring him (telling him secretly in his heart) that one day his brothers' plan would be exposed.
- The brothers returned to their father, tears in their eyes.

- They brought Yusuf's torn shirt in their hands and covered it with animal blood.
- They told him that a wolf had eaten Yusuf when they were playing.
- He didn't believe them, but he told them he had complete faith in Allah and that, with His help, he would see Yusuf again.

Think about it

Why did they come up with the lie that "a wolf ate him"?

God's Scheme

- Although the brothers wanted to kill Yusuf or at least send him far off somewhere, Allah had a different plan for Prophet Yusuf.
- Allah said in the Quran multiple times that no one can change His plan when He makes it.
- A caravan (traveling group) found Yusuf alive in the well. They took him with them.
- They wanted to sell him for a good price in the slave market. In those times in Egypt and other places, young boys were sold as slaves in the market so they could serve their masters.
- This was very common with the prisoners of war and their children.
- The chief minister of Egypt (known as Aziz) bought him and adopted him as his son.
- Aziz liked him a lot, and Yusuf stayed with his family.
- He grew up into a strong, knowledgeable, and handsome man.
- Allah kept him in this land so that he would learn the interpretation (telling the true meanings) of dreams and grow up to be a mighty Prophet of God.

A Test from God

- Aziz's wife became interested in Yusuf because of his beauty.
- She tried to make him sin with her.
- With God's help, Yusuf avoided her and said no to her.
- However, she insisted on forcing Prophet Yusuf. Allah saved Prophet Yusuf because he was a good person and always wanted to obey Allah.

- When Aziz entered the room, his wife tried to blame Yusuf and demanded that he be sent to jail.
- Yusuf explained it was his wife's plan.
- The Aziz believed Yusuf after seeing the evidence that she tried to pursue him.
- She continued until Yusuf made a dua to Allah to send him to jail.
- Allah wanted to save Prophet Yusuf from this evil, so He created such a situation in the palace that Aziz decided to send him to jail.

Staying in the Jail and Two Dreams

- Yusuf met two inmates (people locked up) in the jail who mentioned their dreams to him.
- They liked Yusuf for his kind nature and asked him to interpret their dreams.

Yusuf told him he would serve wine to his master and would be set free.

Yusuf told him he would be hung from a stake where he would die, and birds would eat from his head.

- Yusuf asked the first inmate to inform his master of him (to get some relief).
- But the inmate forgot, and Yusuf stayed in prison for several more years.
- Because Allah had a different plan for Prophet Yusuf.

The dream of the King

- One day, the King had a dream. "Seven fat cows are eaten up by seven skinny ones, and also seven dry ears of grain eating seven green ears of grain."

- The wine pourer remembered Yusuf after no one could interpret the dream. He goes to Yusuf in prison and asks him to tell the meaning of the King's dream. Prophet Yusuf told him:

- People of Egypt will plant grain for seven years straight. So, let them save the corn they grow (leave the grains in their ears) and only eat what they need. Then there will be seven years of hardship (drought), and they will eat all of the corn they saved. Then there will be a lot of rain and celebration the year after that.

- Basically, through this interpretation, Yusuf told them how they could save themselves from years of hardship about to come.

Yusuf wants justice

- When the King heard it, he got interested and wanted to meet Yusuf.
- But Prophet Yusuf wanted the King to make sure everyone knew the truth, why he was in jail in the first place, before he left jail.

- Everyone in the city said they had nothing but good things to say about him; he was a good person who did nothing wrong.
- The Wife of Aziz admitted that Yusuf was telling the truth, and she was the one who did terrible things to him to send him to jail.

Power and Respect

Storehouse

- Prophet Yusuf knew that people would starve if the food was not planned properly.
- He asked the King to put him in charge of the storehouse; the King appointed Yusuf as a Minister in Egypt.

- During the seven good years, Yusuf prepared for the time when the famine would come. He managed the job very well. During the years of famine, Egypt was prepared and had plenty of food. They also helped nearby cities and families by providing food.

Brothers of Yusuf met him

- One day, Yusuf's brothers also showed up to collect the food. They didn't recognize Yusuf, but Yusuf immediately recognized them. They introduced themselves and their family back home.
- He gave them their ration of food, but told them if they wanted more, they should bring their younger brother, Bin Yamin, with them.
- Yusuf ordered his servants to secretly put the money back into his brothers' bags so that, when they returned home, they would want to come back.
- On the next trip, they asked their father to let them bring Bin Yamin with them to get more food.
- Prophet Yaqoob told them that he had already lost Yusuf, but finally agreed after they promised to protect him.

Why was it so important that Prophet Yusuf wanted first to prove his innocence?

The Royal Cup

- When they arrived again, Yusuf told Bin Yamin about himself.
- When they were about to return, as a token of love, Yusuf put a royal gold cup with their luggage so his brother would remember him.

- At the same time, someone announced that the King's measuring cup had been lost, and whoever found it would get more food.
- Upon searching for the King's measuring cup, they found the royal gold cup that Yusuf had placed in Bin Yamin's luggage.
- Since no one was aware of it, they thought that one of their brothers had tried to steal it.
- According to the law of the land, the King announced that the thief would be forced to serve as the King's servant. Yusuf was pleased with this punishment.
- In a way, Allah helped Prophet Yusuf keep his beloved brother with him.

The grief of Prophet Yaqub

- The brothers asked Yusuf to please take one of them in place of Bin Yamin, as they had promised their father.
- Yusuf told them he would be fair and take only Bin Yamin, since he was the one who had the Royal Cup.
- The brothers decided that the oldest brother would stay with Bin Yamin as well.

- The brothers told Prophet Yaqoob upon their return, and he responded that he had patience and faith in Allah.
- He was hopeful that Allah would bring everyone back. It is said that in his grief, he lost his sight.
- The brothers returned to Yusuf and pleaded for the supplies, even when they had few coins.
- Prophet Yusuf felt pity for them, asking, "Do you remember what you did to Yusuf and his brother in your ignorance?"
- They were shocked! And asked, "Are you Yusuf?" Prophet Yusuf said Allah has truly been gracious to him

Generosity of Prophet Yusuf

- The brothers admitted their sins and apologized to Yusuf.
- Yusuf forgave them! He prayed to Allah to forgive them, too.
- He gave them his shirt and said to put it on their father so he could regain his sight (it was a miracle).
- The brothers returned to their father and gave him Yusuf's shirt, and he regained his sight.

- He told them, "Didn't I tell you Allah had told me things you don't know about?"
- They asked for forgiveness, too, and their father forgave them.

The dream came true!

- Yusuf's family travels to Egypt, and they all prostrate to Yusuf out of respect.
- His dream finally came true! The sun and moon were his parents, and eleven stars were his brothers.
- Yusuf tells his father how kind Allah had been to him when he was alone, guiding him all this time and making him the interpreter of dreams.

Lessons Learned

- What do you think of Yusuf's brothers' behavior?
- What do you think about Yusuf's behavior toward them?
- Which evil quality in human being make them do bad deeds?
- What are some of the lessons we can take away from Prophet Yusuf's story?
- What are some of the lessons we can take away from Prophet Yaqoob's story?
- What lessons can we take away from the brothers' story?
- Patience, patience, patience … the ultimate reward is huge!

God reminded us in Surah Yusuf that surely whoever is mindful of Allah and patient, then certainly Allah never discounts the reward of the good-doers.

Chapter 14

The Story of Prophet Shoaib

In this chapter, we will learn about Prophet Shoaib (AS) whose nation was destroyed because of their polytheistic beliefs and dishonesty.

Prophet Shoaib (AS)

Madyan – the City of Prophet Shoaib

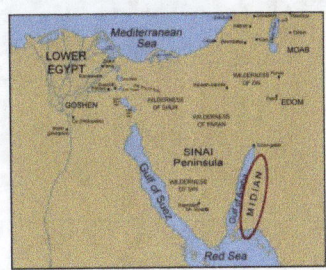

- Prophet Shoaib lived in Madyan on the coast of the Red Sea.
- Many ships crossed the sea, bringing traders from outside with beautiful things to sell.
- The people of the city were intelligent and skilled traders who made a lot of money.
- Prophet Musa also moved here for ten years before prophethood.

Their Problem

- Because of their wealth, they became very proud and forgot about Allah's teachings.
- They used to charge high prices, collect a toll tax from people passing through their land, and measure goods dishonestly – basically, cheating other people in business.
- They were idol worshippers also, so no fear of Allah because they thought the idols would save them.
- Allah raised Prophet Shoaib from among them. This is the practice of Allah that He always sends Prophets from among the nation, so they are not strangers to their nations.
- Prophet Shoaib was one of them, so he warned them about this behavior and practice and told them to fear Allah.
- They ignored Shoaib and even threatened to kill him.
- They made fun of him, saying, "Why does your Salah not want us to make money?"
- Although that's exactly why we pray Salah: it reminds us of Allah and helps us avoid evil.

Why was cheating a big deal?

Dishonesty and Cheating   **OR**   **Honesty**

- Prophet Shoaib warned them about the two evils they were involved in:
    - Polytheism (Shirk) – worshiping other than Allah
    - Cheating others in business
- The first evil is against Allah, and the second evil is against other humans.
- Allah holds us accountable for not only crimes against Him but also crimes against other humans.
- Also, this kind of behavior spreads mischief in any society and ultimately destroys it.
- It was the responsibility of Prophet Shoaib to advise them as their brother and warn them as the Prophet of Allah.

The Punishment

- They did not listen to Allah and His messenger and were ready to punish Shoaib for his sincere advice and for causing "troubles" in their businesses.
- Only a few people accepted the message of Prophet Shoaib and agreed to help him in this cause.

- As happens with the nations of all Messengers, Allah decided to punish them when they rejected the message and the messenger.
- Allah caused a big earthquake that crushed the people of Madyan to death.
- Allah asked Prophet Shoaib to leave the town and take with him those who accepted the message. That way, Allah saved Prophet Shoaib and those few people who believed in him and his message.
- Everyone else died as a result of the big

What happens in a society where cheating on each other becomes common?

Honesty

- We must be honest because other people have put trust in us without saying anything – they assume we are honest.
- If we are not honest, we can never be trustworthy (no one will believe in us for anything).

- People usually think of honesty related to business, but honesty can be extended to many things:
  - Buying and selling – business
  - Homework (think about how we can break the trust?)
  - Leadership
  - Assignments/Exams
  - Contracts
  - Advice/Counsel

Lessons Learned

- Human beings are connected through a shared set of rights and responsibilities.
- Justice means giving each person what they deserve.
- Cheating others in business dealings or taking undue advantage of them is entirely against justice.
- In Islam, there are rights/duties that we have to fulfill towards Allah SWT, and there are rights/duties that we have to fulfill towards Allah's creations – being just and fair with them is one of their fundamental rights.
- Allah SWT will hold us accountable on the Day of Judgment, even if we escape it in this world.

Discuss examples from your life in which honesty can lead to suffering, yet you must still be honest.

Chapter 15

The Story of Prophet Musa (AS)

In this chapter, we will learn about the story of Prophet Musa (AS) in the Quran. A Prophet who is mentioned more than any other Prophet in the Quran.

- Do you know that Prophet Musa is mentioned 136 times in the Quran? More than any other Prophet of Islam.

- Do you know what Egypt is famous for?

Prophet Musa before Prophethood

Egypt at the time of Musa

- In ancient history, the rulers of Egypt were called Pharaohs.
- Musa and many other prophets were from the Children of Israel, the later generation of Yusuf's brothers.
- Pharaoh at that time was a tyrant (cruel leader) who oppressed the Children of Israel. He used to consider himself a god.
- In those times, the people's religion was usually that of the king.
- For him, the life of a person who is from the Children of Israel had no value.
- Musa was born in Egypt during such a difficult time.

The birth of Musa and his mother's test from Allah

- The Pharaoh was torturing the Israelites (the Children of Israel) in Egypt during that time.
- His magicians and fortunetellers (who tell the future) told him that one born among the Israelites would end his rule someday.

- Out of fear, he had given the order to kill all male kids among the newborns of the Israelites every other year.
- He used to spare girls, and when they grew up, he made them servants in the palace.
- Musa's mother gave birth to him amid this order, but she did not tell anyone about the birth.
- She was afraid and worried that if Pharaoh's people found out about Musa, they would take him away and kill him.
- While the mother of Musa was thinking how to hide Musa, Allah had revealed to Musa's mother that when she fears for Musa, she should cast him in the river (in a basket).
- Allah promised to return Musa to her and make him a messenger.

- Musa's mother had a strong faith in Allah, so she put her baby in a basket and cast him into the river.
- Her heart was full of fear and sorrow, although she had a firm belief that Musa would come back to her as promised by Allah.

Allah fulfilled His Promise

- The older sister of Musa followed his path in the river.
- The basket continued to float down the river until it reached the Pharaoh's palace.
- The kind wife of Pharaoh (Aasia) picked up the basket and discovered the child. She adopted him with love.
- When the Queen needed a woman who could nurse the baby, Musa refused to suckle any woman in the palace.
- Musa's sister told them she knew a woman who could suckle the baby – Musa's mother.
- As per His promise, Allah arranged for Musa's mother to be given this chance to reunite with her baby son.
- Remember, Prophet Musa has not yet been made a Prophet.

Musa – A young adult

- The nation was divided into two groups due to Pharaoh's actions—the followers of Pharaoh and the Children of Israel. The children of Israel were slaves in that land and had no respect.
- Musa grew into a strong, knowledgeable, and wise young man.

- Allah has told us in the Quran that He never breaks His Promises, but one must believe in it.
- What is the biggest promise that Allah has made to those who will believe in Him and be good in this life?

- He always wanted to help the weak and the oppressed and could not tolerate injustice committed in front of his eyes.
- He once noticed an Egyptian and an Israelite (one of the people from his nation) fighting in the street.
- He tried to stop the fight, and, in that process, he accidentally hit the Egyptian with a hard blow, and the man died!
- This was a complete accident, as Musa had no intention of killing that person.

Escape to Madyan

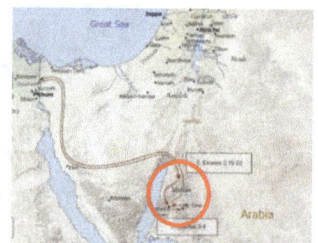

- Due to his sympathies for the Children of Israel, Prophet Musa was already a target of Pharaoh.
- After this incident, Musa realized that although this was a mistake, the Pharaoh would not go unpunished.
- Musa found out that the Pharaoh was planning to punish him with death!
- A well-wisher advised him to leave the country, and he would not get any justice in the court.
- He decided to leave Egypt to the east, towards Madyan near the Red Sea.

Should Prophet Musa run away or face the royal court or Pharaoh? What do you think?

Helping the girls

- When Musa arrived in Madyan, tired, hungry, and exhausted, he rested near a well under a tree.
- He saw two young women waiting to water their sheep flock while some men were at the well - he realized they needed his help.
- They complained that their father was old and the men at the well were not allowing them to take water for their animals.

- He gave them a helping hand, taking their sheep to the well for them.
- He came back under the tree and prayed to God for help.

Marrying the girl he helped

- Allah answered his dua immediately.
- At that moment, one of the women approached him and said that her father wanted to see him.
- The young lady suggested that his father hire Musa for shepherding and other chores for the following reasons:
  - He is strong because he helped them.
  - & honest because he did not ask for any favors in return.
- The father offered his daughter in marriage to him, which he gracefully accepted.

What happens when we make dua?

- Prophet Musa made a dua to Allah for help, and Allah answered it immediately. However, in our lives, we see that it does not happen all the time. Let's first learn the beautiful dua that Prophet Musa made:

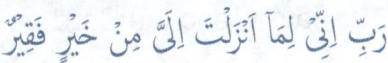

"My Lord! Whatever good you may send down to me at this time, I am in desperate need of it."

- When we make dua, three things might happen:
  - Dua is answered immediately or with some delay.
  - Dua is kept with a reward for the Hereafter because granting it was not good for you.
  - Allah diverts evil from you.
- So, making dua in all circumstances is good.

Staying in Madyan

- The father set a condition for his daughter's marriage to him that Musa would stay in Madyan for at least eight years, if not more.
- Musa accepted and stayed in Madyan for eight years.
- His family grew, and he had kids, too.

Prophet Musa after Prophethood

Allah spoke to Musa

- After serving in Madyan for 8 years, Musa decided to return to his homeland, Egypt, with his family.
- On his journey to Egypt, he traveled through the desert until he reached Mount Sinai, where he realized that he had lost his way.
- He noticed a fire in the distance, so he asked his family to stay there while he sought guidance. This is when Allah spoke directly to Musa and told him he had been chosen as a prophet.
- This was a unique experience for Musa, and that's why he is also known as "Kaleem Ullah" (the person to whom Allah has spoken).

His Miracles

- Allah had a plan to send Musa to Pharaoh with a heavy task, so He decided to give him miracles to protect him, his family, and the Children of Israel.

 Allah told Musa to throw the staff he had been using onto the ground. The staff turned into a huge snake. Allah told Musa to grab it without fear. When Musa did so, it returned to his original staff.

 Allah ordered Musa to put his hand under his armpit and remove it. Musa's hand came out shining brightly with a strange light coming out of it.

Huge Task

- Allah told Musa to go to the pharaoh and give him Allah's message – the two signs (miracles) given to him would protect him from Pharaoh.
- He was tasked to take the Children of Israel out of Egypt to a different land.
- Musa asked the pharaoh to leave his cruel and unjust practices toward the Children of Israel and set them free.
- He showed him signs, but the Pharaoh didn't listen, and his opposition and cruelty only increased instead.
- He debated about Allah and declared himself a god above any other god.

A duel with the Magicians

- The Pharaoh ordered the best magicians to duel (compete) with Prophet Musa.
- He was thinking that his nation's great magicians would teach Musa a lesson, as he told them he would reward them generously if they won.
- Prophet Musa asked the magicians to throw their sticks first. The Magicians threw down their sticks, and they appeared to have turned into small fake snakes – Musa was initially afraid.
- But, as magicians always do, it was all fake and appeared to people as snakes, not the actual snakes.
- Then Musa threw down his staff, and it turned into a real giant snake that ate all of their fake snakes and the sticks together.
- The miracles given to the prophets by Allah are real, not magic.

Magicians

Prophet Musa

Magicians believed

- The Magicians knew this was real, not a trick.
- They bowed down to Allah and said they believed in the God of Musa.
- They realized that what Musa had done could not be done by any human being on their own, and God must be behind it.
- The Pharaoh became furious!
- He told them they would be executed if they didn't take back what they said.
- The Magicians prayed to Allah to give them patience and to let them die while believing in Him.
- This type of change can only be brought by a true Prophet and his teachings.
- This was a sign for Pharaoh and his people to believe in one True Allah, but they did not learn anything.

More Warnings for Pharaoh and his people

- After this, Allah showed more signs to the Pharaoh and his people to see if they would finally submit to Allah.
- The following signs from Allah with them:
    - A severe drought and a flood.
    - Attack locusts, lice, and frogs (in the form of rain)
    - A river of blood appeared in the city.
- After each sign, the people and Pharaoh would beg Musa to ask Allah to forgive them and stop the sign. Musa would pray to Allah to bring things back to normal, but the Pharaoh would go back to his evil ways.

The Punishment from Allah

- Allah ordered Musa to leave Egypt with his people.
- The pharaoh decided to pursue the fleeing slaves along with his entire army.
- The Children of Israel were trapped between the Red Sea in front and the pharaoh's army behind.
- Allah inspired Musa to strike the sea with his staff. Suddenly, the sea parted to reveal a dry pathway that Musa's people walked across.
- The pharaoh and his army also took this path to the middle of the sea, where it returned to its original form. The pharaoh and his army drowned.
- At the time of his death, Pharaoh claimed that he believed in Allah, but it was too late.

- After Pharaoh and his people were drowned and the Children of Israel got freed, Allah asked Prophet Musa and the Israelites to go and settle in the land of Palestine.

Lessons Learned

- When a person has strong faith, they believe in Allah's promises and in what they have been asked to do.
- Human beings make their plans, but the best planner is Allah.
- Allah also rewards us for the good deeds that we do in this world.
- When we are on the wrong path, Allah gives us many warnings to fix our acts.
- Arrogance is our worst enemy, keeping us away from every good.
- Everything happens for a reason, and if we trust Allah, especially in difficult situations, we will have a more peaceful and happier life.

Chapter 16

The Story of the Cow and Children of Israel

In this chapter, we will learn about the story of the Cow and the Children of Israel mentioned in Surah Al-Baqarah of the Quran.

The Story

A crime was committed

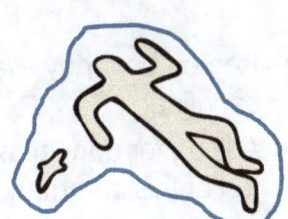

- This story is mentioned in the Quran in Surah Al Baqarah, which is why it is called that. Al Baqarah in Arabic means the cow.

- The Children of Israel had forgotten Allah's favors and were not following Allah's teachings anymore.

- They were involved in all kinds of social evils.

- One time, a murder took place in the community, and someone among them committed that.

- No one wanted to admit to the crime committed in the community.

- Allah decided to expose the criminal in a unique way.

Slaughter a cow

- Upon Allah's command, Prophet Musa asked them to slaughter (killing an animal for meat) a cow.

- They were told that if they struck the corpse (dead body) with the cow's flesh, the dead man was to wake up and name the killer miraculously (it would be a miracle from Allah).

- The Children of Israel knew that Allah wanted to expose the criminal. So, they used the old technique: avoid doing what has been asked.

- They started asking irrelevant questions to avoid slaughtering:
  - O' Musa, are you joking with us because Allah cannot ask for such a thing?
  - What type of cow should it be?
  - What color should it be?
  - How old?

- These questions had nothing to do with what Allah had asked them to do. Allah asked them to do something very simple: "Slaughter a cow."

- They could have just slaughtered any cow, and Allah's command would have been fulfilled.

- But their main objective was to avoid doing it.

Attitude Problem

- The Children of Israel had lost faith and started questioning everything, down to the smallest detail, while missing the main things.
- They were ungrateful and complained constantly.

- Remember, they even asked Prophet Musa if he was mocking them about the sacrifice.
- Asking for unnecessary details about the cow was a sign that they were making fun of this command from Allah.
- Finally, the Children of Israel did slaughter a cow, but not willingly.
- Once they slaughtered the cow, Musa found the murderer through the miracle that Allah promised. The murderer was punished for the crime he committed, and that's what Children of Israel was trying to avoid.
- Because of their attitude towards Allah and His Messenger, He punished them by wandering (lost) in the desert for another 40 years.

Lessons Learned

- When it comes to Allah's commands, we should follow them without asking unnecessary questions.
- That does not mean we should not make efforts to understand the command.
- Allah made this religion very easy for us, but sometimes we make it difficult by asking unnecessary questions.
- Follow the order of Allah and put in your best efforts.
- For every order of Allah, the real objective of the command must be kept in mind.

Discuss examples of situations in which asking too many irrelevant questions can make things difficult, rather than simply doing what was asked.

Chapter 17

The Story of Ashab e Kahaf

In this chapter, we will learn about one of the Quran's most interesting stories about young people who accepted Islam and faced challenges as a result.

Surah Al Kahf

- Surah Al Kahf is a unique Surah of the Quran that contains four very unique stories. The Surah is named after the first story in that Surah.

- Surah Al Kahf was revealed in Makkah just before the Prophet migrated to Medinah when the persecution (ill-treatment) of Muslims was at its peak, and the Prophet was going through a tough time.

- The four stories contain lessons for both Muslims and disbelievers.
- Prophet Muhammad advised us to read this Surah frequently to learn from it and to keep our faith strong.

Four Trials and Four choices

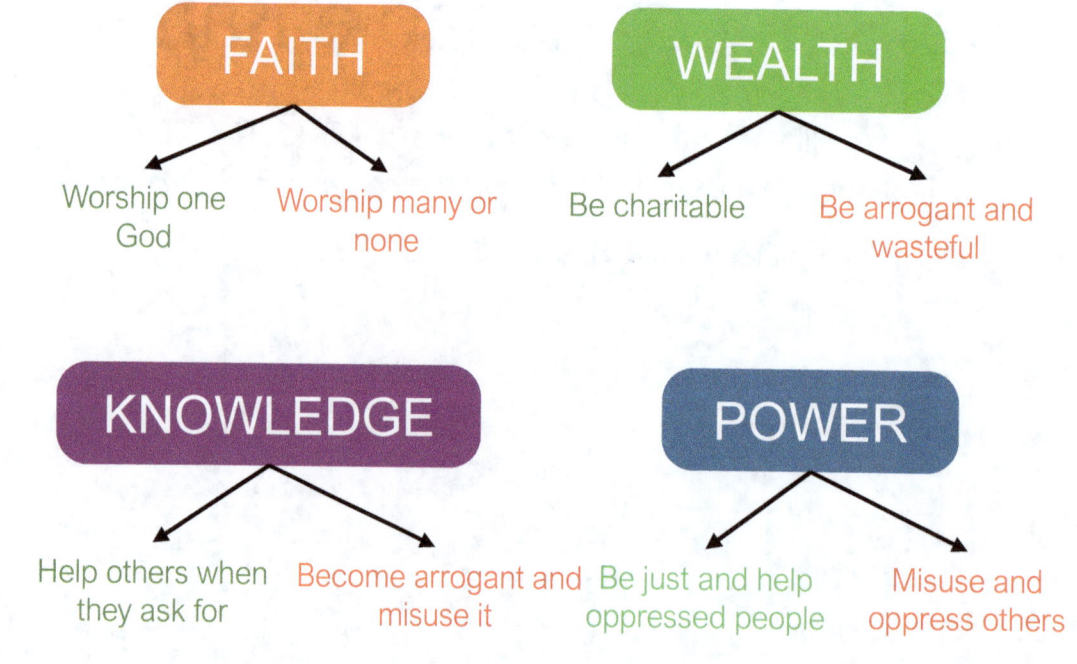

FAITH
- Worship one God
- Worship many or none

WEALTH
- Be charitable
- Be arrogant and wasteful

KNOWLEDGE
- Help others when they ask for
- Become arrogant and misuse it

POWER
- Be just and help oppressed people
- Misuse and oppress others

Take one trial from the four trials and discuss how it can be a test for us.

People of the Cave

The Trial of FAITH

Muslim Youths and their Test

- In the books of history, these few youths were also known as "Seven Sleeper" (the Quran did not mention their number).
- They used to live in a town near Turkey and were followers of the teachings of Prophet Jesus.
- The King was not happy with the teachings because, at the time, the King was considered a god on earth, and all the people were supposed to worship him.
- These youths used to believe in one true God (earlier followers of Jesus were Muslims).
- The King wanted them to leave Islam.
- After much effort, the King failed to convince the youth.
- He decided to punish them.
- It was a big test for the youth as they might lose their lives to protect their faith in Allah. Remember, the test of faith is the biggest faith.
- They still decided not to obey the King and told everyone that they would continue to worship Allah alone without any partners.

Allah's help for the youth

- When the King asked his men to arrest the youth so he could punish them, they found no choice but to run away from the city.
- They found a small cave on top of a mountain and hid there. The cave is located outside the city of Ephesus, which is now in modern-day Turkey.
- They thought they would go back when King's men stopped looking for them.
- They asked Allah for help and prayed that Allah would keep them on the straight path.

O' Our Lord! Have mercy on us from yourself, and guide us in this matter of Ours."

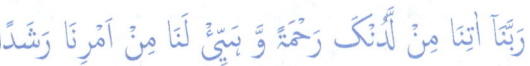

رَبَّنَآ اٰتِنَا مِنْ لَّدُنْكَ رَحْمَةً وَّ هَيِّئْ لَنَا مِنْ اَمْرِنَا رَشَدًا

Allah saved the youth

Wikipedia

- Allah saved them in a unique way.
- Sleep took over them, and they slept for hundreds of years without anyone noticing.
- Allah took care of them while they were sleeping.

- Their dog stayed outside the cave during this time.
- Allah asked the angels to turn their sides during sleep.
- The cave was positioned so sunlight did not enter directly, and it remained slightly dark, but the heat did.
- Some say they slept for 309 years, but the Quran is silent on the matter.

The youth woke up

- When Allah awakened them, they tried to figure out how much time they had slept.
- They discussed among themselves, and some said they slept maybe a day or part of a day.

- They were all hungry, so they sent one of the youths to buy food. He took the coins they had to buy the food. In those days, coins bore the King's image.

People found out

- The youth appeared as a stranger immediately.
- His clothes were in a style that hadn't been worn for centuries.
- The city had changed so much that he had to ask people for directions.

- The person sounded strange when he talked with the merchant (language issue).
- The coin he tried to use had a picture of the King from centuries ago.
- It turned out the silver coins were hundreds of years old!
- They became talk of the town in no time, and everybody started talking about these "strange" youths.

Why were they debating that they slept for a day or less than that, although they slept for a long time?

Allah honored them

- After some investigation, the people of the city recognized who they were because, after they had disappeared, they became a tale.
- Now, everyone in the city was following the teachings of Jesus, and they were all Muslims.
- Soon, the youths died, and the people of the city honored them by making a mosque near their graves.
- They did not lose hope in Allah, and Allah miraculously saved them.

Lessons Learned

- Faith in Allah is the greatest treasure you have.
- Your faith is your identity; no matter where you are, never compromise it.
- If you are strong in faith, Allah's help is sure to come – He will find ways for you that you cannot think of.
- If your life is in danger due to faith, it is your duty to protect it.
- Good company is always helpful when it comes to protecting your faith – choose your friends wisely.
- Hard times do not last forever; they are here to pass.
- Do your best, and then keep your trust in Allah.

In the story, Allah did not mention the city's name, the number of youth, or the years they slept. Why?

Chapter 18

The Story of the Two Gardens

In this chapter, we will learn about the story of two men who had an interesting conversation about Allah and the gratitude that we should show towards Him.

The Owner of the Two Gardens

The Trial of WEALTH

- As mentioned earlier, Surah Kahaf has multiple stories that provide different lessons. This story of the two gardens is about how wealth and the blessings of Allah can become a test for people.

The story of two men

- This story is about two men: one rich with a large family, the other poor with a small family. In those days, a large family was considered part of wealth, especially the boys, because they used to earn money for the entire family.
- In the story, they are having a conversation about life and the blessings of Allah.

A Rich Person

A Poor Person

- Allah blessed and tested the rich man with two gardens of grapevines, date palms, and other types of crops.
- There was a river flowing near the gardens, making them rich in produce.
- Both gardens produced a lot, which made him rich. He was also blessed with many children.
- On the other hand, Allah tested the poor man by leaving him without enough.
- He did not have many children either.
- Both of these situations are just tests. None of these situations tells us about their relationship with Allah.
- Most people think that if they have more blessings from Allah, then Allah is happy with them, and if they lack Allah's blessings, then Allah is not happy with them. That's a complete misunderstanding about this life.
- Allah tests people by giving them more, and sometimes by giving them less than others.

Their conversation

- When it was about to bear fruit, they had a talk about life and the blessings that Allah had given them.
- The rich man boasted about his rich gardens and the other blessings he had, thinking he had earned them through his efforts.
- He said that he does not believe in the Hereafter and that "And if there is such a thing," then he will be rewarded more because Allah seems to be happy with him.
- He thought his riches were due to Allah's happiness with him and his efforts.
- The poor man was so surprised to hear from the rich man. He replied that rejecting the Day of Judgment is like rejecting Allah.
- The poor man said that he was convinced that Allah is the creator of everything and He will hold us accountable (we will be asked about it) one day.
- He advised the rich man to be grateful to Allah for everything he has and to use these blessings to help His creation.
- He hoped that Allah would give him riches and children one day because all of this comes from Allah.
- He warned the rich man that Allah does not like arrogant people, and He might punish him for this in this world and the Hereafter if he does not believe in Him the way He deserves.
- The poor man was sincere to the rich man and wanted him to change his behavior so he could continue to enjoy the blessings of Allah. The rich man ignored his advice.

Punishment and Regret

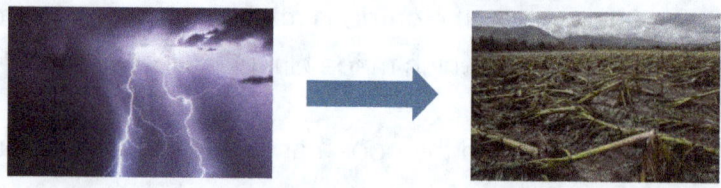

- A heavy cyclone/storm in the area destroyed the gardens and fruits of the rich man. The rich man found himself helpless when he saw the destruction because he did not truly believe in Allah and never asked for His help.
- He regretted his situation:
  - For being arrogant because of the riches given to him by Allah.
  - He boasted about his wealth and looked down on others.
  - Not realizing that we are not in control of this life and what's around us, it is Allah alone.

Lessons Learned

- We should be grateful to Allah at all times, whether we are rich or poor.
- Sometimes, lack of wealth becomes a blessing for you – you don't forget Allah while busy in your worldly life.
- A believer should attribute every blessing and goodness to Allah, even if you put all your efforts into getting something, but if Allah does not want it, you will never get it.
- Being rich in this world is a big test, not a sign that Allah is happy with us.
- Arrogance is your worst enemy; it will destroy all your good deeds.
- When a sincere friend gives you good advice, listen to the advice and act on it.
- The best way to be thankful to Allah is to share your riches with others.
- Sometimes Allah punishes people in this world for others to take lessons from, but mostly Allah leaves people in their conditions, sends them warnings, and takes them to task on the Day of Judgment because this life is a test.

A believer who Allah keeps poor in this life will have a big advantage on the Day of Judgment. Can you think of a reason why?

Chapter 19

The Story of Prophet Musa and Khidr

In this chapter, we will learn a very informative story about Prophet Musa and Khidr, who had a specific type of knowledge from Allah.

The Story of Prophet Musa and Khidr

The Trial of Knowledge

- This is the third story that is mentioned in Surah Kahaf.
- Through this story, God wants to teach us that sometimes what appears to us does not give us the complete picture. Things happen for a reason and as God planned. If we trust God in matters beyond our control, we will be rewarded with better results for our patience.

Prophet Musa meets Khidr

- Allah had Prophet Musa travel very far to meet a knowledgeable and wise person whom Allah had given special knowledge of the unseen.
- Prophet Musa traveled with his servant in a boat to find the person.
- Allah told him that they would find this person near the junction of two rivers, where the fish for lunch would come alive and jump into the river in front of their eyes.
- Prophet Musa's companion witnessed the event but did not inform Prophet Musa until he asked for the fish for lunch.
- They traced back to the same place where fish jumped into the river and found the person.
- In Ahadith, it is mentioned that his name was Khidr.
- Some historians also think he was an angel in the form of a man, sent by Allah to teach something.

Prophet Musa wants to follow Khidr

- Prophet Musa asked the man if he could follow the man on his journey and learn from him.
- The man said strange events would occur, and he would allow Prophet Musa to follow if he promised not to ask any questions.
- He said that Prophet Musa won't be patient enough to learn from him.
- Prophet Musa promised to be patient in the journey and not ask any questions.
- The man agreed, and they set out on the journey of knowledge.

First Incident – The Boat

- They set out on the journey and found a boat along the way. They boarded the boat, but the man made a hole in it!
- Prophet Musa was confused. "How could you drown these people while the boat owner has given us a favor? This is horrible!"
- The man said, "I knew you would not be patient with me."
- Prophet Musa apologized and said he would not do it again.

Second Incident – The Boy

- They continued to travel and found a boy.
- Musa noticed that the man had suddenly killed the boy.
- Musa was confused and shocked. "How could you kill an innocent boy? This is horrible, and you've done something very evil!!"
- The man said again, "I knew you would not be patient with me."
- Musa apologized and said he would not do it again. He said if he questioned him again, the man could tell him not to travel with him.

Third Incident – The Falling Wall

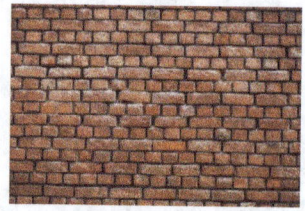

- They continued their journey and entered a town.
- They were tired, so they asked for a place to stay and some food, but the residents refused.
- Musa and the man went outside the city, where an old wall was about to fall.
- The man started to repair it, but Musa told him not to, because the town's people were not good with them.
- The man said again, "This is the end of our journey. Now I will explain why I did what I did."

The reality of incidents

- Initially, Khidr only asked Prophet Musa to stay quiet and observe without asking any questions. Then later, Khidr explained the incidents himself:

The Boat

"The boat belonged to some poor people. There was an evil king who would take all of the good boats. So, I damaged it so the king wouldn't take the ship, but the poor people could repair it easily and continue earning their livelihood."

The Boy

"The boy would turn out to be a bad son who would give grief to his parents, who were true believers. So, I killed him as Allah would give them a better, more caring son in his place."

The Wall

"The wall belonged to two orphans who lived in the city. A treasure lay beneath it, but they needed to be older and more mature to take it. So, I repaired the wall so there was more time for them, and the people of the town wouldn't take it knowing that they were greedy people."

- The way Khidr handled these incidents suggests that the man was an angel who appeared as a human being.
- Angels are usually assigned for these types of tasks; they perform without us knowing, and we see them as incidents in our lives.

First Reaction Exercise:

Share your first reaction to the following situations. Be honest:

1. You are born into a poor family, while most of your cousins are from rich families.
2. You prepared well for your cousin's marriage, but missed your flight on the day of the marriage.
3. One of your friends' brothers was not a safe driver, and he recently died in a car accident.
4. Your father is hard-working, and his coworkers are jealous of him. He lost his job today.
5. You did not want to move out of the city where you were born because of your friends, but your parents decided to move to a different state for a better job opportunity.

Lessons Learned

- When a person has strong faith, they believe in Allah's promises and in what they have been asked to do.
- Human beings make their plans, but the best planner is Allah.
- Allah also rewards us for the good deeds that we do in this world.
- When we are on the wrong path, Allah gives us many warnings to fix our acts.
- Arrogance is our worst enemy, keeping us away from every good.
- Everything happens for a reason, and if we trust Allah, especially in difficult situations, we will have a more peaceful and happier life.

Chapter 20

The Story of Dhul Qarnain

In this chapter, we will learn about one of the mightiest kings who ever lived on earth, Dhul Qarnain.

King Dhul Qarnain

The Trial of Power

Who is Dhul Qarnain?

- Dhul Qarnain means 'Master of two horns' because he conquered the nations of the Persians and the Medes.
- His name in history is Cyrus the Great, who was a Persian king (529 BCE).
- Although some historians think Dhul Qarnain was not Cyrus, but another king in history.

- In a few years of rule, he ruled over all the nations around him, from East to West. No other king had such a huge kingdom.
- He was a faithful servant of Allah and a very just ruler.

Why is Dhul Qarnain mentioned in the Quran?

- Quraish were not aware of this figure in history, but Jews were.
- Jews asked Quraish to ask Prophet Muhammad about Dhul Qarnain as a test of Prophethood.
- Cyrus the Great helped the Jews gain freedom from the Babylonian king's slavery.
- He helped them rebuild Jerusalem and the Temple of the Doom.
- Jews used to admire him.

Reconstruction of Jerusalem by Cyrus: The Bible, Book of Ezra, 1921.

- The Quran, through the Prophet Muhammad, told the Jews about Dhul Qarnain exactly as they were expecting.
- Jews still did not believe in Prophet Muhammad.

How can power and leadership become a test for you?

A believing king

- Dhul Qarnain was an honest and just king who believed in one God and the Hereafter.
- He lived during the time of Zoroaster, a monotheist.
- That's what made him a just king, always ready to help people.

JUSTICE

- Dhul Qarnain believed in all the Prophets of the Children of Israel.
- Despite his power over people, he told those under his rule that he would punish only the oppressors.
- Allah tested Dhul Qarnain by giving him power and authority over people to see how he would use it.

He helped many nations

- The Quran describes many journeys that Dhul Qarnain took, during which he helped people with their problems.
- In one of his journeys, he found a nomadic (who do not settle in one place) and uncivilized (don't have a culture) nation that used to live in the open.
- They were attacking neighboring nations, causing significant problems for peace in the area.
- Dhul Qarnain fought them and took control.

Wall built to stop Yajuj Majuj

- In his other journey, he found a group of people living near a pass between two mountains.
- They were speaking a strange language, and it was hard to understand them.
- They, somehow, explained to him that the tribe of Yajuj and Majuj was spreading evil in the land.
- Yajuj Majuj are the children of the third son of Prophet Nuh, the Yapheth.
- They offered him wealth to build a wall in the pass to protect them from the mischief of Yajuj Majuj.
- He refused to take any wealth and asked them to help him build a wall of Iron slabs and molten brass, which made it stronger.
- Instead of boasting about his capabilities, he said this was a blessing from Allah and that it would be broken when Allah wished.

Yajuj Majuj aka Gog Magog

- Yajuj and Majuj are the third generation of the children of Prophet Nuh.
- They were wild and uncivilized and used to attack civilized nations in that area and loot their wealth.
- They were prevented from doing that by the wall.

- However, the Quran and the Bible both predicted that they would soon come out of this isolation (living alone) period and would rule the world in the end times.
- According to some historians, the Mongols were the same people who emerged from hiding and conquered much of the world, and now their descendants are ruling in the US, Australia, Europe, and Canada.

Lessons Learned

- Allah tests people with different things: wealth, poverty, sickness, power and authority, beauty, and many others.
- In this world, every person has a different test.
- Once we understand that our abilities and what we have are a test, then we should be careful in our behavior.
- The best behavior in this world is to avoid arrogance and to attribute all blessings and situations to Allah when things are beyond our control.
- We should take responsibility for what we can do.
- The signs of the end times are described in the Quran and other books to strengthen our faith in Allah when we see them unfold.

Chapter 21

Prophet Dawood (AS)
Prophet Sulaiman (AS)

In this chapter, we will learn about two mighty Prophets who were also Kings among the Children of Israel, and Allah granted them many miracles.

Prophet Dawood (AS)

The history of the Children of Israel

- Allah chose the Children of Israel to present His religion to other nations on earth.
- For that, He sent many messengers, among them, including Musa, Yusuf, Yaqoob, Dawood, Suleiman, and many others.
- As a nation, they were asked to be settled in the land of Palestine and make it their home.
- They fought many wars to establish their rule over Palestine.
- When one of the Prophets urged them to fight for their land, they asked Allah to choose a king who could lead the fight.
- Allah chose Talut, a strong, young, and energetic man from among them, as their leader or king.
- As usual, Bani Israel was not very happy with this choice because Talut was from a poor family.

Dawud, the Warrior

- In one of the important battles against the Children of Israel, the Canaanites fought under their fearless, strong leader, Jalut (Goliath).
- The Children of Israel became afraid of his presence and refused to fight.

- Only a handful of believers at the time decided to fight the army of Jalut, among them Dawood (who was not a prophet).
- They said that if Allah is on our side, then this small group of people can defeat the army of Jalut.
- Their dua is reported in the Quran: "Lord! Bless us with patience; make our standing firm and make us win over these disbelievers."
- With a slingshot, Dawood knocked the giant warrior Jalut to the ground and then killed him with his sword.
- The army of Talut then defeated the enemy and eventually made the area a secure country.

Dawood, the Prophet King

- When Talut died, people made Dawood their king.
- Dawood was a just and kind ruler, so Allah blessed him with His prophethood.
- As a warrior, he knew how to make the best armor, made of iron, for his army, and with Allah's help, they became a powerful army that was hard to defeat.
- Jerusalem was also conquered in his time.
- Allah praised Dawood in the Quran for his wisdom, righteousness, and gratitude to Allah, even though his kingdom was far and wide.

The Psalms (Zaboor)

- Allah gave Prophet Dawood the Zaboor.
- He had a beautiful voice, which he used to recite the verses of the Zaboor.
- When he would recite the verses of the Zaboor, Allah ordered the birds and mountains to recite with him.
- It is said that every creation of Allah praises Allah in a way that we cannot understand.
- Zaboor (the Psalms) is part of the Bible today – it is a collection of praises of Allah and supplications (duas).

Dawood was tested

- One day, two people showed up in his private chamber, where no one was allowed.
- They were arguing over a matter: one of them had one sheep, while the other had ninety-nine.
- The one with only one sheep complained that the other person was rich and powerful and asked for the only sheep he had to be handed over to him.
- The rich man was good at speaking, and because of his position, people supported him.
- Prophet Dawood did not like it and chastised the rich man. As soon as he did so, the two men disappeared, and Dawood realized he had made a mistake.
- It was a test for him, and those people were angels.
- He immediately turned toward Allah, prayed, and asked for forgiveness.
- Allah loved Dawood greatly for his humility.
- The Quran does not mention what mistake Dawood made. The Quran mentioned this story to show how humble Prophet Dawood was. As soon as he realized his mistakes, he was ready to ask for forgiveness from Allah, although he was a king.

Prophet Sulaiman (AS)

Prophethood and Kingdom

- Two Prophet kings are mentioned in the Quran who were among the Children of Israel. We already learned about Prophet Dawood.
- It's very unique that a king is also a Prophet of Allah.
- After the death of Prophet Dawood, his son Sulaiman became the king of the Israelites.

- Allah made him also a prophet. He was kind-hearted and gentle. Allah gave him knowledge, wisdom, and the ability to administer justice.
- He ruled a vast kingdom but never forgot to pray to Allah and submit to Him.
- He made a dua to Allah that he should hold a kingdom unlike any other in history. So, Allah gave him unique capabilities, including the ability to understand the language of birds; they also served in his army as messengers.

Miracles of Prophet Sulaiman

Control over Jinns

- One of his miracles was that Allah had given him control over Jinns (a powerful creature made of smokeless fire).
- They used to work for him, doing all sorts of things.
- They used to construct giant palaces, chambers, and bowls for him, all with Allah's permission.
- They also used to dive into the sea to bring pearls to Sulaiman.
- Remember, he made a dua that his kingdom would be unlike any other.

Control over Winds

- The Quran states that Allah made sailing easy for his ships to trade during the most ideal times.
- That could mean either that Allah gave him control over the winds above the ocean or that Allah commanded the winds to help him in his sailing.

- This allowed his ships to travel faster and in the directions he wanted. This made his journeys shorter, even for distant places.
- This made his kingdom flourish economically and also militarily.
- Even today, the ideal conditions of oceans and winds for sailing are considered the biggest advantage a sailor can have.

Talking to animals

- He once came across a valley of ants while marching with his army.

- The ants panicked and said to each other, "Be careful or Suleiman and his armies will accidentally crush you!"
- Prophet Suleiman heard this and smiled, then prayed to Allah that he and his people would always be grateful for the blessings Allah had given them.
- He instructed his army to remain careful when passing through the valley of ants and to stop if necessary.
- Hoopoes served in the army, and Prophet Sulaiman used to have regular conversations with them.

Kingdom of Sheba

- The Kingdom of Sheba was possibly located in southwestern Arabia, now part of Yemen.
- Prophet Sulaiman learned from the messenger Hoopoe about a kingdom of Sun worshippers called Sheba.
- Sheba was ruled by a Queen who had a magnificent throne.

Creation of Allah

- Prophet Suleiman sent a letter with the bird to the Queen.
- In the letter, King Suleiman told the Queen and her people to stop worshipping the Sun because the Sun is just a creation of Allah. Only Allah should be worshipped alone.
- The Queen was surprised and didn't want any trouble with Prophet Suleiman, given his powers, so she sent a bunch of gifts in return.

Bringing the throne of the Queen of Sheba

- Prophet Suleiman sent a return message telling her angrily that Allah has given him everything he needs and more, and he doesn't need their gifts.
- Prophet Suleiman asked his ministers, "Which one of you can bring me her throne the fastest?"
- One of the jinns said, "I can bring her throne here faster than you can get up from your throne."
- But one of the more knowledgeable companions said, "I can bring it here faster than you can blink your eye."
- When the throne was brought in, Prophet Suleiman instructed them to disguise it so that she would not recognize it.
- When she arrived, they asked her if it was her throne, and she was surprised to see it there.

Queen of Sheba accepts Islam

- The Queen of Sheba was amazed by the palaces of Prophet Sulaiman and by his humility.
- Prophet Sulaiman had asked the jinn to make a palace made out of glass and crystal before the queen arrived. He told her to enter it.

- When she entered, she thought there was water on the floor, so she raised her dress to keep it from getting wet.
- When Prophet Suleiman told her it was made of crystal, not water, she realized the truth.
- She was amazed by the blessings Allah had given to Prophet Sulaiman. She prayed to Allah, "I have wronged my soul! Now I fully submit to You, Allah."

Temple of King Sulaiman

- With the help of the hardworking Jinns, Prophet Sulaiman also built a temple for worshiping Allah, famously known as the Temple of Solomon or the Dome of the Rock.
- After Jews changed the Islamic practices that Prophet Sulaiman and Dawood gave them, the famous Al-Aqsa Mosque was later built near this temple.

- The whole area is called Bait Al-Maqdas (The sacred house). For Prophet Sulaiman, the Dome of the Rock was the mosque where he used to worship Allah, much like Muslims pray in a mosque.

Prophet Sulaiman's death

- Prophet Sulaiman died while sitting on his throne, as the jinns were working on construction projects.
- His body sat upright on the throne, balanced on his staff.
- The jinn thought he was still alive, so they continued working until they finished.
- The termites ate his staff, and he collapsed. They realized that Prophet Sulaiman had died a long time ago.
- If the jinn had known that Sulaiman had died, they would have left the work incomplete and fled.
- He is buried in a mausoleum in the basement of the Temple.

Lessons Learned

- There is nothing wrong with enjoying the blessings of this world, including rulership, as long as the person is humble and fears Allah in every matter.
- Every creature in this universe praises Allah by obeying Him. Sun, moon, clouds, birds, and animals simply follow what they have been told to do and do not disobey.
- Everyone makes mistakes, but what is important is that, once you realize the mistake, you ask for forgiveness from others (if you have wronged them) and from Allah.
- If the Quran does not mention something in a story, we should learn the lesson from it and leave it alone rather than pursue it.
- All the miracles that are given to Prophets, like talking to animals, are all given by Allah, and it all happens with the permission of Allah.
- No one knows the future, not even the Jinns.

Chapter 22

Harut and Marut

In this chapter, we will learn about two angels from the time of Prophet Sulaiman who became a test for the Children of Israel.

Harut and Marut

Prophet Muhammad and the Jews

- The Torah predicted the coming of the Prophet Muhammad, but they refused to believe because they were expecting the last prophet of their generation.
- The Jews of Arabia were not willing to believe in anything that Allah sent down through Prophet Muhammad.
- When Prophet Muhammad went to the Jews with his message, a group of them acted as if they had never heard of the news in the Torah about the last prophet before.
- They were very jealous of Prophet Muhammad.
- They even became enemies of the one who brought Allah's revelations (the Quran) to Prophet Muhammad -- the Angel Jibrael.
- Ideally, they should be the first to accept Allah's message.

Prophet Suleiman and Magic

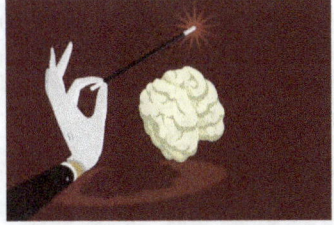

- The Jews tried to harm him by reaching out to their wizards, who taught magic and satanic practices, claiming that these came from Prophet Suleiman.
- In magic, you may rely on Jinns (devils), and a Prophet would never commit such acts of disbelief.

- Magic is disbelief because people who exercise it do not maintain their faith in Allah and start looking to other beings to fulfill their desires, fair or unfair.
- It was the devils who were guilty of disbelief.
- They accused Prophet Suleiman because Allah gave him power over some Jinns.
- To harm Prophet Muhammad, some Jews wanted to learn the magic that angels Harut and Marut used to teach thousands of years ago in Babylon.
- Powerful magic can affect the human body and soul.

Why is magic bad and can lead people to disbelief in Allah?

The magic of Harut and Marut

What was the magic?

- Harut and Marut were two angels whom Allah sent as a test for the Jewish people – they may have come in the form of humans.
- They might be teaching unique words (chants) or charms used by Jewish Saints and Preachers.
- This chant/charm was used to ward off the evil eye, witchcraft, or magicians.
- The magical chants can be used in different ways. For example, some magical chants can harm certain people, and others can benefit people.
- The evil eye means that jealous people can harm you in terms of your health or wealth.
- It was also used to create love or hatred between people.
- It did not involve polytheism, and there were no jinns or devils.
- But it was just as strong as the magic and witchcraft that Jinns did.
- Allah may have taught this chant/charm (magical rhymes) to the Israelites when they were slaves in Babylon.
- It was taught because magic and sorcery were so powerful in Babylon, and ordinary people had no way to protect themselves against them.

The effect

- People started misusing the chant/charm, despite the fact that Harut and Marut warned them that this is a test from Allah and that it must not be used to harm people.
- Through this, they would try to create hatred between husbands and wives.

- A good relationship between a husband and wife is the foundation for a stable and happy society.
- If this relationship is disrupted, it can cause a society to fall apart.
- When society starts to fall apart, chaos ensues, and people stop caring for each other.
- Angels told them that they were committing a big sin.

Lessons Learned

- Any magic is considered prohibited in Islam for the reason that it makes you depend on the creation of Allah, like Jinns, people, and Satan.
- Some chants and charms might be helpful and have a positive effect on the human body and soul, but most of the time they are misused to harm people; it is therefore recommended to stay away from them.
- This is not like science, where you can always predict the effect of something.
- People who play any role in separating a husband and wife without a valid reason and who cause a rift between them commit a serious sin.
- Some people have the power to have a positive impact on you through their words – for example, powerful speakers.

Chapter 23

Prophet Yunus (AS)

In this chapter, we will learn about a unique Prophet, Prophet Yunus, whose famous dua is mentioned in the Quran.

Prophet Yunus (AS)

The City of Nineveh

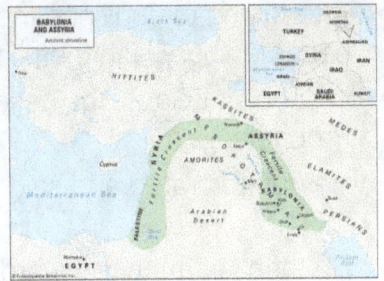

- Prophet Yunus lived 3,000 years ago in the city of Nineveh, on the banks of the Tigris River in Mesopotamia, which had a population of more than 100,000.

- The area was settled as early as 6000 BCE and, by 3000 BCE, had become an important religious center for the worship of a few famous goddesses.

- The ruins of ancient Nineveh lie directly across from the modern city of Mosul (in Iraq today).

- At its peak in the 7th century BC, it was the largest city in the world.

- Kings ruled this city, one of the largest and richest of the time.

- It had a powerful army, which also made them arrogant.

The people and their culture

- The culture of Nineveh was very rich, and its people were proud of it.

- Most of the people were idol worshippers.

- The moral situation towards the Creator and the creation was not very good.

- The city's rulers liked to spend money on themselves rather than their people.

- Idol worship leads people to lose their morality.

- Prophet Yunus, son of Matta, was among them a righteous servant of Allah.

- He began to tell people to give up idol worship, serve only Allah, and live a good and clean life.

- But almost everyone ignored Prophet Yunus' message!

- Like every other Prophet, he also approached the nation's leaders. In those days, the leaders always influenced their people's beliefs about religion.

- Allah also sends his prophets to large cities, which are the centers of civilization. Nineveh was one of them.

Why does Allah send his messengers to large cities, which are centers for people?

Prophet Yunus gave up

- After trying to convince them of the truth, Prophet Yunus became angry with them for not listening.
- In such situations, the nation's leaders also usually threaten their Prophets.
- He got frustrated and said he hoped Allah's wrath would befall them.
- He then left the city towards the Persian Gulf.

- He gave up on his mission too early and did not want to return to Nineveh.
- He considered his efforts a hopeless cause and wished Allah would destroy them already. Prophet Yunus, instead of remaining steadfast, gave up.
- Prophets and Messengers of Allah are not allowed to act on their own. They must wait for Allah's instructions for everything.

Allah punished Prophet Yunus for his impatience

- The Prophets get their share of punishment in this world when they make mistakes – it is not left for the Day of Judgement.

- It happens because they are the role model for their nation, so Allah tells them immediately if they have done something wrong and corrects it.

- He boarded a ship to get away from the city that was caught in a big storm.

- To prevent the ship from sinking, the captain ordered some people to jump overboard to lighten the ship and make it easier to sail.

- They did a random drawing (called lots), and Prophet Yunus' name came up.
- He was thrown off the boat as a result.
- As soon as Prophet Yunus was thrown into the sea, the winds began to die down.
- Prophet Yunus was swallowed by a gigantic whale.
- He managed to survive by keeping his head afloat in a pocket of air inside the whale.
- He was inside the stomach for around three days and three nights (or maybe more).

Dua made for the help

- He soon realized that only Allah could save him.
- Yunus had taken Allah's decision into his own hands!
- He knew he was being punished and being taught a lesson.

- He cried out to Allah, begging for forgiveness. Allah heard him and forgave him.
- The whale swam to the seashore and spat Yunus out of its belly and into shallow water. Allah caused a squash plant to grow over him to provide shade and keep insects away.

لَّا اِلٰهَ اِلَّا اَنْتَ سُبْحٰنَکَ اِنِّی کُنْتُ مِنَ الظّٰلِمِیْنَ

["Lord!] There is no deity except you. Exalted are you. Indeed, I was unjust to myself." (21:88)

Guidance comes from Allah

- When Prophet Yunus returned to his nation to continue his mission, he found that they had amended their ways.
- Allah decided not to punish them.
- His teachings continued to affect them after he left the city.

- He realized that his job was to deliver the message and tell people what is right – Allah will guide people based on their intention, and sometimes we don't know their intentions.
- It is said that Prophet Yunus' nation was the only nation that avoided the punishment of Allah by accepting the message of the Messenger.

Lessons Learned

- Our job is to deliver the truth about anything (religion or outside) and tell people about what is right and what is wrong.
- Allah did not make us responsible for the people. We should perform our task without considering the results.
- The guidance comes from Allah – we CANNOT guide people.
- Patience is key when you are doing the right thing – giving up is not an option.
- This dua that the Prophet Yunus made is very powerful, and we can use it even in difficult situations.
- Prophets are our role models in every situation.

Chapter 24

Prophet Ayyub (AS)

In this chapter, we will learn about Prophet Ayyub, whose patience is considered an example for everyone.

The Prophet Ayyub

- Prophet Ayyub lived in northern Arabia, somewhere near Palestine.
- He was from the generation of Prophet Ibrahim and was sent among the Children of Israel.
- His time was around 900-1000 years before the birth of Jesus.
- He gave Allah's guidance to people.
- Allah does not talk much about him in the Quran, and we have very little information about him from other authentic sources.

The Children of Israel received many prophets among them.

His Wealthy Life

- Prophet Ayyub was a wealthy and well-respected figure among those around him.
- He had a lovely, large house, family, cattle, farms, and other blessings of Allah one could imagine.
- His life was enjoyable and full of pleasures, for which he was very grateful to Allah, and he used to thank Allah often.
- At the same time, he was a very generous and kind person who used to worship Allah a lot.
- The jealous people around him used to say that he was only a grateful servant of Allah because he had been given too much.
- They claimed that he would not be closer to Allah if he had nothing.
- This is the problem with jealousy. People find excuses to bring other people down.

What is jealousy, and why is it bad for someone who is jealous? Do you remember an example of jealousy in one of the Quran's stories?

The biggest test of his life

- Allah decided to test Prophet Ayyub with one of the greatest tests a human being can face.
- He lost everything he had one by one, including his children and wife.
- He lost his health also and got a bizarre, gross disease.
- Because of the nature of this disease, everyone left him alone.
- His love for Allah was so great that he associated all this pain and suffering with Satan because it was he who incited jealousy among people who did propaganda against him.
- Even in this situation, he remained grateful to Allah and never complained to others about it.
- Ayyub's patience is famous and is used as an example in many cultures.

His Dua to Allah

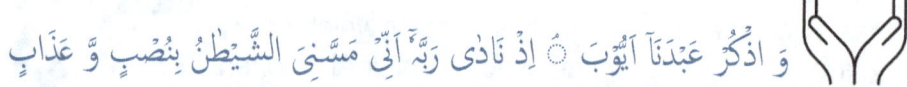

وَ اذْكُرْ عَبْدَنَآ اَيُّوْبَ ۘ اِذْ نَادٰى رَبَّهٗٓ اَنِّیْ مَسَّنِیَ الشَّیْطٰنُ بِنُصْبٍ وَّ عَذَابٍ

And remember Our servant Ayyub when he called his Lord: "Satan has inflicted me with great sorrow and pain (so help me)." (Surah Saad: 41)

Here comes Allah's help

- After thoroughly testing him and proving people wrong about Prophet Ayyub's faith, Allah decided to remove all his difficulties.
- Allah restored his health through a stream under his foot that cured all his diseases, and he used it for drinking and bathing as well.

- Allah gave him back his family, but this time twice as many as before.
- Allah also returned his wealth and livestock to him in greater abundance.
- Allah tells us in the Quran that Ayyub passed the test and was patient and grateful.

Lessons Learned

- This life is a test – we are tested when we have many of Allah's blessings, and when we don't.
- We should make due to Allah to make our tests easier.
- We should be grateful when we receive a blessing, and patient when we lose it.
- There is nothing wrong with complaining privately to Allah about your situation – we should not complain publicly and act impatiently.
- Allah does not test people beyond what they can tolerate.
- There is always some relief at the end of every suffering.
- Our best tools in these situations are Salah and Patience.

Chapter 25

Prophet Isa (AS)

In this chapter, we will learn about Prophet Isa (AS), whose life is nothing short of a miracle.

Which group worships Jesus (because they think he is the son of God?

Prophet Isa (AS)

Maryam – the mother

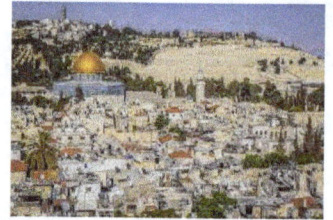

- Prophet Zakariah was appointed as the caretaker of Maryam, the mother of Prophet Isa.
- She was dedicated to the House of Worship even before she was born because her mother vowed to dedicate her newborn for the sake of God.
- She used to spend her time only on religious activities and duties.

- She started spending more and more time with Prophet Zakariah and became a very religious and wise woman.
- It is important to note that some Christians consider Maryam as the mother of God, which is not true because God cannot have parents or children.
- Prophet Zakariah realized something special about Maryam as she was close to Allah even when she was young.
- Allah always spoke very highly of her in the Quran.
- The mother of Maryam made a dua for her protection from Satan before her birth.

Angels gave the news

- Because of her love for the place of worship, Maryam never married.
- But Allah decided to give her a good child miraculously – without a father.
- Only two people in history were born miraculously, Prophet Adam and Isa.

- A few angels came in the form of men to greet her.
- She became afraid of them; the angels told her they were the messengers of Allah and wanted to give her good news.
- They told her that she would bear a good child, Isa, who would be the last prophet sent to the Children of Israel.
- She was shocked; angels told her that when Allah decides to do something, He says "Be," and it happens.

A Test for Maryam

- It was a big trial for Maryam, who was worried about how she would explain the birth of her child with no father.
- To escape from the people, she hid in a remote place.
- At the time of birth, she was hungry, and Allah told her to shake the palm tree, and fresh dates would fall from the tree.
- At the same time, a stream of fresh water came out from the ground near her, so she drank from it.
- Allah told her that if someone asked about the baby, she should, through signs, tell them she was not talking to anyone.
- Instead, Allah asked her to point to the cradle of Isa.

Prophet Isa Spoke

- When Maryam pointed toward Isa, people got confused; how would they talk to a baby?
- Baby Isa spoke miraculously:

Credit: Getty Images/iStockphoto

"Indeed, I am the servant of Allah. He has given me the Book and made me a prophet. And He has blessed me wherever I am and has commanded me to pray and give Zakah as long as I am alive. And [made me] good to my mother, and He has not made me a pitiful tyrant. And peace is on me the day I was born, I will die, and the day I am raised alive." (Surah Maryam)

His unique miracles

He talked while still in the	Healed the sick.
Cured the	Cured the	Feed many poor

Gave life to the dead, including giving life to clay birds.

Saved by Allah when the Jews tried to kill him.

Raised by Allah with his body after his death.

He taught wisdom

- Prophet Isa was asked to follow the laws given in the Torah.
- He also preached the Torah to his nation.
- However, they used to follow it without knowing the wisdom (reasons) behind its verses.

- This made their attitude towards religion very rigid and hard. Hence, they lost many instructions from Allah because of that.
- They introduced many new things in the religion that Allah did not approve.
- The Bible, which is the history of Prophet Isa, is full of wisdom.

A piece of wisdom

Understanding the wisdom (reasons) behind a command helps us follow it easily. For example, many Muslims pray without understanding why, and it becomes a burden to them later. Keep in mind that Allah looks at the intention behind our actions and at how sincere we are in them.

His nation's leaders tried to kill him

In those days, death on the cross was the official way of punishing someone.

- The common people loved Prophet Isa because of his kind and loving nature, his miracles, and his wisdom.
- The rich and scholars did not like this attention towards him, and they became his enemies.
- Due to his miracles, given by Allah, they called him an "imposter" who was acting as a Prophet.
- They feared losing control of the ordinary people.
- The rich made a false case against him before the Roman Emperor, who ruled over Palestine.
- They blamed Prophet Isa for an uprising (armed fight) against the Romans.
- The Roman police tried to capture Prophet Isa and punish him for a crime he had never committed.

Allah saved Prophet Isa

- Remember, one of the Sunnah (practice) of Allah is that He does not allow His Messengers to be killed by his enemies.
- When the Roman police came to arrest Prophet Isa, he went into hiding.
- One of his students betrayed and informed the police about his whereabouts.
- Allah miraculously put Prophet Isa's appearance on that person's face, and all the students thought he was Prophet Isa.
- Roman police arrested the person who betrayed Prophet Isa, thinking he was him.
- That person was crucified (put on a cross hanging), and everyone thought they had killed Prophet Isa.
- The Quran clearly states that they never killed Prophet Isa, but it was made appear so to them.

Wrong beliefs about Isa (Jesus)

- Because Allah saved him and the Jews could not kill him, the companions of Isa (Jesus) found him alive on the third day after his presumed crucifixion.
- The companions considered it a huge miracle and considered his 'coming back' a godly act.
- All the wrong beliefs about him being God or the Son of God began because of this reason.
- However, it is hard to say exactly when people began worshiping him.

Lessons Learned

- Every prophet of Allah is our prophet, and He gave something special to each one of them.
- Prophet Isa was the last in the chain of prophets sent to Bani Israel; that's why Allah gave him many unique miracles to convince them of Allah's Power.
- Miracles are from Allah; the Prophet, on his own, cannot do anything.
- In Islam, there is wisdom behind every instruction; we may not understand it at first, but if we learn it, we will be able to find it.
- No enmity or personal benefits should stop us from accepting the truth.
- If we have strong faith in Allah's power, He can save us from harm.

Chapter 26

Prophet Zakariah (AS)

In this chapter, we will learn about Prophet Zakariah (AS), who took care of the mother of Prophet Isa.

Prophet Zakariah

His Family

- He was a descendant of Prophet Harun.
- He was also Maryam's uncle.
- His family used to take care of the house of worship in Jerusalem.

- He was a very dedicated servant of Allah, worshiping Allah most of the time.
- Many stories are common between the Quran and the Bible. There is more detail about his life in the Bible; however, the Quran avoids going into every detail.

Caretaker of Maryam

- He was also the caretaker of Maryam when her mother dedicated her to the house of worship.
- They cast a lot regarding the caretaker of Maryam, and Prophet Zakariah was chosen.
- Maryam would only spend time on religious activities. Since Prophet Zakariah was a very religious man, she spent much time with him, which is why she became a very pious and wise woman.
- Whenever Prophet Zakariah visited her in her worship chamber (room), he noticed the blessings of Allah showered on her, including the wisdom in her conversation (plus non-seasonal fruits).
- There was a lot of wisdom in her talks, and Prophet Zakariah was so impressed with this young lady and felt happy about her upbringing.
- On time, Prophet Zakariah asked her about all these blessings. He asked, "Where do you get this from?" She said that this is from Allah because of her strong belief in Allah.

Blessing is everything we have; it is not just food and clothes. The religion of Islam, family, money, free time, health, ability to think … all are blessings from Allah.

Dua for children

- Zakariah also did not have children, but he wanted one.
- When he saw the blessings of Allah upon Maryam, he desired, once again, a child like Maryam.
- He made dua to Allah for a good child who will continue his practices and take care of the house of worship of Allah.

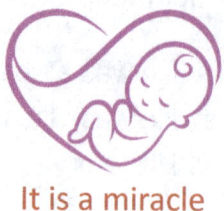

It is a miracle

- He was of old age at that time, and his wife could not bear children, but Allah finally answered his dua.
- One day, angels gave him the good news of Prophet Yahya, a prophet, a leader, and a person who would not marry and dedicate his life to Allah.
- Prophet Zakariah was confused by the angels' appearance, so he asked for a sign. As a sign, Allah told him that he would not be able to speak to anyone except to praise Allah.

Prophet Yahya

- Allah named him Yahya when the angels brought him the news that he would be a prophet, which makes him unique.

- It is a great honor for someone when Allah names them. Prophet Yahya was one of them.
- It is interesting to note that both Prophet Yahya and Prophet Isa were Prophets of Allah, and their births were miracles.
- Prophet Yahya grew up to be a very devoted, religious, and wise person.
- Like many other prophets of Allah, Prophet Yahya followed the Torah's teachings and guided others toward it.
- The Quran mentions that he was wise from a very young age.
- He was very kind to his parents, who brought him up in his old age.
- He decided to dedicate his life to Allah's message and to teaching it to others, to the point that he remained single and never married.
- It is said that one of the kings among the Children of Israel tortured and murdered him. Killing a human being is a big crime, but killing a prophet of Allah is a way more serious crime.

Lessons Learned

- Allah grants wisdom to those people who are closer to Him in the relationship.
- We must make dua with the belief that Allah will listen to our dua – Allah only delays the response, when necessary, sometimes until the Day of Judgment.
- Anything is possible for Allah – He created the physical laws in this world, but He can break them whenever He wishes.
- The greatest blessings in the world are guidance from Allah and the wisdom and patience required to maintain them.

Chapter 27

The story of the revelation of the Quran

In this chapter, we will learn about a different story, which is not about a Prophet but about the miraculous revelation that a Prophet received.

The Quran

What is Revelation?

- Revelation means the messages that Allah sent to a person on earth directly (to a person's heart) or indirectly through an angel. The messages are meant to guide the person and those around him on various matters, especially religion.
- Some revelations were written as a book; the Quran is one of them.

Do you know any other revelation that is written as a book?

Why did Allah give us the Quran?

- Many prophets were given holy books; Prophet Muhammad was given the Quran.
- The Quran is in the Arabic language and is given to Muslims and all humanity alike.
- After Prophet Muhammad, we now have to rely on the Quran for guidance.
- The Quran is like a scale (balance) that decides on every matter of religion.
- In matters of Islam, the Quran is the final word.
- Allah has sent every Holy Book for the same purpose.
- With the Quran, we should judge what is good and what is evil.

What does it mean that the Quran is a scale?

- When something is a scale, the answer to every religious question is first checked there, rather than elsewhere.
- If it has answered that question, then that is the final answer on that matter.

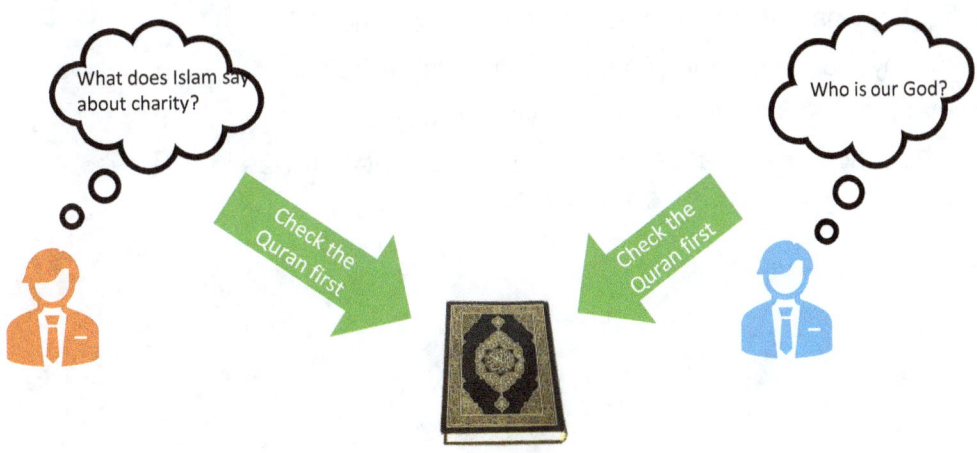

When was the Quran revealed?

- The revelation of the Quran began in the month of Ramadan.
- Prophet Muhammad was 40 years old at that time.
- Allah gave it to Angel Jibrael, Angel Jibrael gave it to Prophet Muhammad, and he gave it to us, as it is.
- Angel Jibrael taught Prophet Muhammad orally, and he memorized it immediately.
- The revelation took 23 years to complete; Prophet Muhammad was 63 years old when it was completed.

The Quran and Ramadan together help us to get closer to Allah.

Allah ➡ Jibrael ➡ Prophet Muhammad ➡ Us

The first revelation

- Before prophethood, Prophet Muhammad saw many dreams (visions) that prepared him to be a Messenger of Allah.
- He saw Angel Jibrael in those dreams with some verses of the Quran; also, one incident is reported in the Cave of Hira.
- One day, Angel Jibrael appeared in the sky directly in front of Prophet Muhammad and told him that he would be a Messenger of Allah.
- Angel Jibrael came close to the Prophet, sat down, and taught him with great attention and affection.
- Some historians say that Surah-e-Fatiha, the first surah of the Quran, was revealed to the Prophet at that time.
- Others say that Surah Alaq was the first Surah revealed.
- However, this is just a matter of studying history.
- After that, the Quran was revealed to the Prophet as it was needed. The entire Quran took 23 years to complete.

Allah called the Quran a light that shows the right path toward God to the people

Prophet Muhammad and the Quran

- The Quran was revealed to the heart of the Prophet Muhammad by Angel Jibrael with Allah's permission.
- He could memorize it immediately as if he would never forget it.
- At the time of revelation, the Prophet used to sweat profusely, as if he were undergoing a very exhausting exercise.

- Angel Jibrael sometimes appeared to him as a human being and taught him the Quran.
- Prophet Muhammad had a team of Scribes (people who write) who wrote the Quran as instructed by the Prophet.
- The Quran was written down on many materials during the Prophet's lifetime.

How Allah Protected the Quran

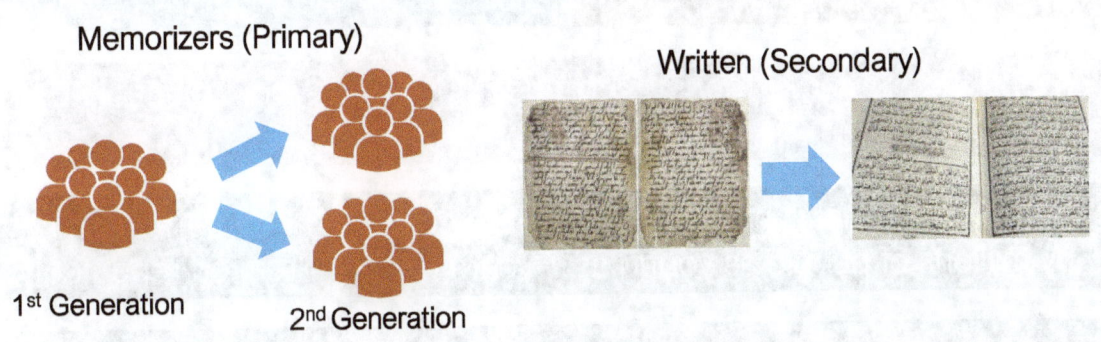

Memorizers (Primary)

Written (Secondary)

1st Generation

2nd Generation

- Allah protected the Quran from the Jinns and Satan at the time of its revelation because the Quran came down from the sky to the earth, and usually Jinns and Satan listen to these types of conversations.
- In the last Ramadan of the Prophet's life, Angel Jibrael reviewed it twice with him.
- Thousands of companions memorized the Quran.
- Since that time, generation after generation has memorized the Quran and transmitted it in its original words and reading.
- Scholars of Islam have studied classical Arabic, and many have mastered it.
- Companions not only memorized the words but also how to read them properly. This did not happen with any other holy book.

Some Facts about the Quran

The current order of Surahs in the Quran is different from the order of revelation. Prophet Muhammad compiled it in a different order.

The Quran is the speech of Allah as He would deliver

It can be read like poetry but its not poetry

Every Surah starts with Bismillah except Surah Tauba

There are 114 Surahs in Quran

Quran was revealed to Muhammad in almost 23 years

The Quran is the most read book in the world

Surah Baqarah is the longest Surah in Quran

Only 25 prophets are mentioned in the Quran

Among the previous prophets, Prophet Musa is the most mentioned in the Quran – 136 times

The only book that is memorized cover to cover by millions of people as young as 7 years old

Quran means "recited repeatedly"

The topic of the Quran is the life story of Prophet Muhammad and his message to the people

Quran is translated in almost every language

There are millions of reciters of the Quran.

The complete Quran is recited in the month of Ramadan worldwide and listened to by more than a billion people.

Thousands of non-Muslims have claimed that they reverted to Islam just by reading the translation of the Quran.

Lessons Learned

- The Quran must be the focus for anyone who wants to learn about Islam.
- Thousands of people converted to Islam because they loved the Quran when they read it for the very first time.
- To introduce Islam to someone, we should give them a copy of the Quran.
- Anyone can read the Quran without making wudu; it's not a requirement.

Recite any surah of the Quran you have memorized to the class.

Chapter 28

The story of Hadith

In this chapter, we will learn about something very dear to Muslims: the historical record of the Prophet Muhammad's life and his practice of Islam.

The story of Hadith

What is Hadith?

- Hadith means the speech of someone.
- In Islam, it means the historical record of Prophet Muhammad's sayings, actions, and approvals.
- The companions loved Prophet Muhammad greatly, so they began observing, writing, and recording what the Prophet said, did, or approved. That's what we do when we like or love someone. It was a natural thing to happen.

Famous Books of Hadith

- Some people were very good at it, and they collected many sayings of the Prophet and shared them with others after his death.
- However, it is important to note that Allah or the Prophet never promised that Hadith would be protected as the Quran is, but the companions and scholars still collected them based on their knowledge. Thanks to them!

What is the role of Hadith?

We follow his path and example

Through hadith, we learn about his life, personality, daily activities, exemplary Islamic practices, character, morals, and statements of wisdom.

- First and foremost, Prophet Muhammad practiced Islam when he was alive. He gave us Sunnah.
    - He prayed 5 times a day.
    - He fasted in Ramadan.
    - He gave Zakah and Charity.
    - He married ……. and so on …..
- The companions recorded all his practices in the form of hadith, and we now have the best examples of how to practice Islam.
- A hadith contains only actions of the Prophet that are already established in Islam through the Quran and Sunnah.
- If a Hadith talks about something strange in the Quran and Sunnah, scholars do not accept it.

How did it reach us?

- We only have so many large Hadith books. But this is not how it all started.
- For the first hundred years, it was mostly transmitted orally.
- Islam was limited to a few countries and regions, and Muslims were honest when it came to transmitting hadith.
- Then people started lying about it to become famous. People who used to tell stories about Prophet Muhammad usually become famous very quickly.
- Islamic scholars took it seriously and transformed this transmission into a science of collecting hadith.
- The aim was to remove made-up stories from the beautiful collection of Prophet Muhammad's sayings and keep it clean and reliable.
- Hadith is a treasure of knowledge given to us by the Prophet's companions and organized by the scholars of Islam, a process that did not occur with any other Prophet in history.

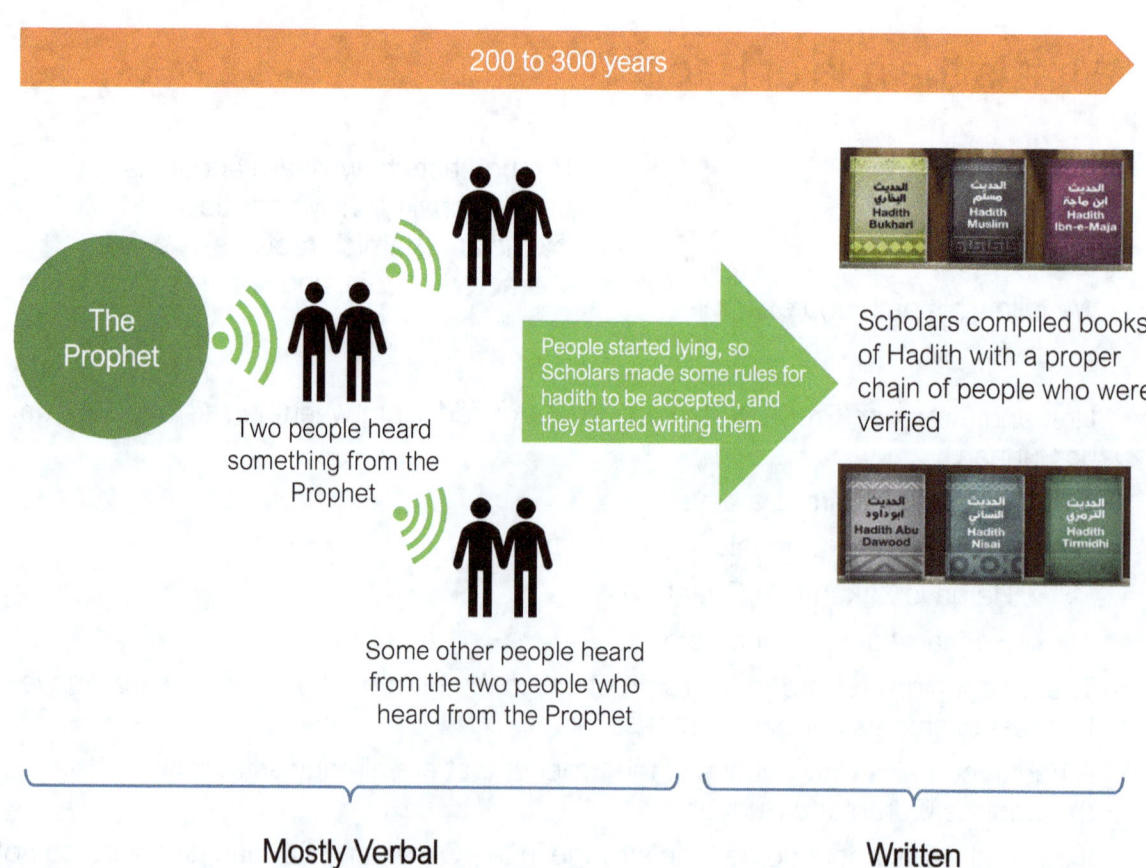

200 to 300 years

The Prophet

Two people heard something from the Prophet

Some other people heard from the two people who heard from the Prophet

People started lying, so Scholars made some rules for hadith to be accepted, and they started writing them

Scholars compiled books of Hadith with a proper chain of people who were verified

Mostly Verbal

Written

The chain of narration

- The chain of narration goes like this:
  - A heard something from Prophet Muhammad
  - B, C, and D heard from A
  - and E, F, G, H heard from B, C, or D
- Notice that many people heard it in the end, but it all started from one person, A.
- For example, in the chain below, it all started from one person, Abu Hurairah.
- It also happens in our daily lives. If you attend a lecture in the mosque, you tell something important you learned to your friends, and they tell it to their friends. Note that it all started with you.

An Example Chain

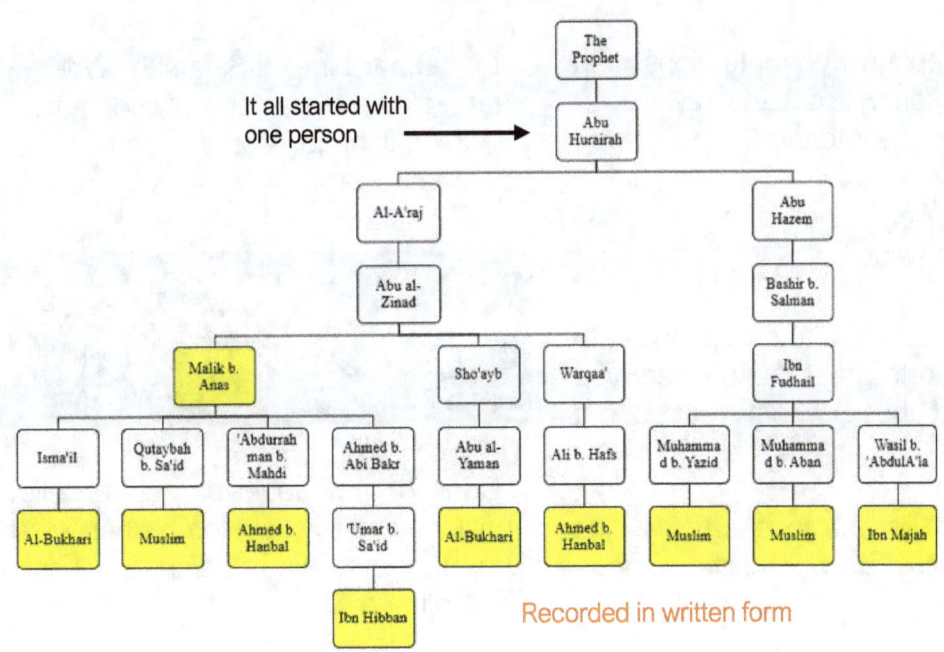

- The scholars of Hadith look for two things when they hear a Hadith:
  - Who reported it? The complete chain.
  - What is reported?
- Every person in the chain is checked thoroughly to see if they are telling the truth.
- The reported saying or action must be consistent with common sense, social norms, the Quran, and the Sunnah.

Seerah of the Prophet

- One of the benefits of Hadith is that historians were able to write the Seerah of Prophet Muhammad.
- Seerah is the life history of Prophet Muhammad.
- Some people have even recorded features of his face, his hairstyle, his height, how he walked, and how he talked.
- Prophet Muhammad is the only personality in the history of mankind whose life is recorded with such detail.

There is much to learn from the life of the Prophet Muhammad.

Some Beautiful Hadith

- Let's look at some hadith that are full of wisdom.

"Deeds depend upon intentions, and every person will get the reward for what he or she intended."

"Oh, Omar bin Abi Salamah! When you eat, take the name of Allah, eat with your right hand, and eat from the side nearest to you."

"The Believer is not stung from the same hole twice."

"The best acts are to share food with others, and to greet those whom you know and those whom you do not know."

"Do not disregard a good deed (no matter how small it may seem) even if it is your meeting with your (Muslim) brother/sister with a cheerful face."

"A Muslim is the one who avoids harming Muslims with his/her tongue and hands."

"None of you would be a true believer until he/she wishes for his/her Muslim brother/sister what he/she wishes for himself/herself"

"Do not hate one another, and do not be jealous of one another, and do not desert each other, and O' Allah's worshippers! Be brothers/sisters. It is not permissible for any Muslim to desert (not talk to) his/her Muslim brother/sister for more than three days".

Lessons Learned

- Like the Quran and Sunnah, Islam also has Hadith, a treasure of knowledge.
- Hadith is studied to know how the Prophet practiced Islam, what he said, and what he approved or disapproved.
- Through Hadith, we learn many words of wisdom from someone who communicated directly with Allah.
- We need to learn the Seerah of the Prophet to know how he led his life.
- The entire religion of Islam is transmitted to us through the Quran and Sunnah, and Hadith only shows us how the Prophet practiced it.

Learn one new hadith and share it with everyone in class next week, and explain what you learn from it.

Chapter 29

The stories of Prophet Muhammad's Character

In this chapter, we will learn a few stories from the life of Prophet Muhammad that show his beautiful character.

Prophet Muhammad's Character

Why should we read about Prophet Muhammad's Character?

- Allah said about Prophet Muhammad in the Quran:

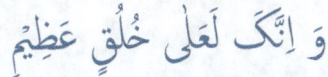

And indeed, you are of a great character.

- One Prophet's wife, Aisha (RA), was asked about the character of Prophet Muhammad. She responded, "His character is the Quran." Meaning he was a walking Quran in his manners and in how he deals with Allah and the people around him.

1 The Quran says that Prophet Muhammad has the best character (person).

2 Prophet Muhammad's character is the best example for us to follow.

3 It increases our love for him, which is required for our faith (belief).

4 It is natural to want to know more about the person whom we love.

5 We take lessons from his life and his moral behavior to emulate (copy).

6 While he was the Messenger of Allah, his personality had many angles. He was a religious and political leader, a family person, a husband, a father, a son, a neighbor, and a common man in society.

7 If we want to get closer to Allah, our best path is to look to Prophet Muhammad and see how he did it because he was closest to Allah.

8 Many non-Muslims who do not know Prophet Muhammad talk negatively about him. The more we know about him, the more we can educate people around us about his character.

Story 1 Importance of Justice (Fairness)

Alliance (Agreement) of the Virtuous

- This happened before the prophethood.
- A man came to Makkah on business and met a Quraishi man, who agreed to purchase his merchandise (goods) and pay later.
- The next day, the Quraishi man refused to pay.
- The visitor went to the leaders of the Quraish and asked for help.
- They ignored him. It was not the practice among Makkans.
- He felt cheated in a visiting land.
- He approached the Kabaah, called everyone, took off his shirt, and recited poetry about the generosity and honor of the people of Makkah.

- He reminded everyone that the visitors expect better from the people of Makkah.
- The Makkans were ashamed of the situation and called a council (group of elders) to discuss the matter.
- Prophet Muhammad joined the meeting along with Abu Bakr.
- Everyone decided to side with the oppressed (the wronged).
- To make sure it did not happen again, they made a pact (written promise) and signed it – it was termed "Hilf al Fudool" (Alliance of the Virtuous).
- The people of Makkah were very sensitive about breaking the pact, and they took it seriously.
- The tribes that actively participated in it were Banu Hashim (the tribe of the Prophet Muhammad), Banu Zahra, Banu Muttalib, Banu Asad, and Banu Taym.
- The pact marked the beginning of a basic justice system in Makkah.

Hadith

Prophet Muhammad said, "I witnessed a pact of justice in the house of Abdullah ibn Jud'an that was more beloved to me than a herd of expensive red camels. If I were called to it now in Islam, I would respond." (Sunan Al Kubra #13080)

Lessons Learned

- When it comes to matters of justice and other goodness, we should join hands with everyone, not just Muslims.
- The people of Makkah corrupted the religion of Ibrahim, but they had many good human qualities that produced people like Abu Bakr and Omar.
- Allah does not like injustice and requires us to stand for justice, even if it goes against our interests or our family.
- Injustices create other evils in society.
- We should protect the rights of the weak in society.

Story 2

Wise Man

Rebuilding Kabaah

- The Kabaah has been rebuilt several times in history.
- When Prophet Muhammad was 35 years old, heavy floods caused much damage to the Kabaah, and the Quraysh decided to rebuild it.
- To protect the Kabaah from floodwater, it was decided to raise the foundation and walls and install a roof.

- It was a blessed task for them, and everyone wanted to participate.
- Every tribe was given a specific duty.
- It was decided that only money from reputable sources would be accepted from all contributors.
- When the Kabaah was almost rebuilt, an argument (dispute) broke out about the placement of the black stone.
- Every tribe wanted to get the honor of putting it back.
- They argued for many days, and there was a danger of tribal dispute.
- Someone suggested that whoever from Quraysh entered next through the Banu Shaybah entrance would be the arbitrator (mediator) in this matter.
- The next person to enter through that door was none other than the man already titled As-Sadiq and Al-Amin, who was appointed the arbitrator.
- Everyone was happy that the best man among them became the arbitrator.

The eastern corner of the Kabaah has a black stone

The significance of the black stone in Islam is merely symbolic. When pilgrims start Tawaf, they kiss the stone or wave their hands towards it as a sign of renewing their faith in Allah.

- Being a wise person, Prophet Muhammad came up with a solution. He asked to bring a sheet of cloth. He laid that sheet on the ground and placed the black stone at its center. He then asked the leaders of all the Quraysh tribes to lift the blanket from its sides and then climbed the wall himself. When the sheet was raised, he took the stone and put it in its place himself.

Lessons Learned

- When you are in a position to decide, be fair and wise.
- We must be sensitive about other people's religious matters.
- Social issues must be handled with wisdom, without hurting people's feelings, while still doing the right thing.
- If you have earned respect among the people around you, they will always trust you.
- Wisdom is a gift from Allah; it is not necessary that only learned people are wise.

story 3

The Prophet of Mercy

Visit to Taif

- Taif and Makkah were considered twin cities.
- Tribal leaders of both cities were known and respected throughout the Arab region. People even married into each other's families.

- The 10th year of Prophethood was the most difficult in the life of Prophet Muhammad because of the death of his wife Khadija and his uncle Abu Talib.
- In the 10th year of Prophethood, after Prophet Muhammad lost the support of Abu Talib, he left Makkah to preach Islam.
- He decided to travel to Taif, hoping people would welcome him because of the two cities' legacy.
- He decided to meet with a few leaders in Taif to explain Islam and seek their support.

- The leaders' response was very disappointing and hostile (harsh).
- They ignored the Prophet and used abusive language toward him.
- He stayed there for a few days, but it did not help.

- When he decided to leave the town, they ordered their mischievous (bad) people to follow, who threw stones at him.
- He got injured as a result, and so did his servant, Zaid, who got hit on his head.
- This was an unexpected response because he was a guest in the town, and Arab tradition holds that guests should not be mistreated. It was possible that Makkans had already told the people of Taif about him and how they should treat him because of their enmity.
- Treating a Messenger of Allah with such harsh treatment is one of the serious crimes and sins.
- On his way back from Taif, the Prophet, and his servant He and his servant took refuge in an orchard. It belonged to a family in Makkah who sent him grapes through their slave, Adas.
- Adas found it strange when he heard the Prophet saying "Bismillah". He told the Prophet that he was from the city of Nineveh.
- The Prophet said that that was the place where "my brother Prophet Younus preached." Upon hearing this, Adas immediately accepted Islam.
- That was the first incident in this journey that showed him that people's attitude determines whether they listen to and accept the message.

Allah sent his help

- The Prophet felt sorrow because of the behavior of the leaders of Taif, and he prayed to God sadly:

"O God, I am weak; my resources are limited, and my efforts are weak. You are the Master of the weak. I have no trust in anyone but You. You will give victory."

- An angel appeared and sought permission from him to crush the city of Taif between two mountains.
- The Prophet restrained him and said he hoped God would bring people within a generation who would worship only one God.
- His vision proved true: in just a few years, the entire city of Taif accepted Islam.
- Allah makes prophets experience something comforting to their hearts in difficult times.
- In Nakhlah, the Prophet was reciting the Quran in a loud voice when a group of Jinns heard the Quran.
- They informed their fellow Jinns about it.
- They said they heard a great and beautiful message about God's oneness.
- Allah revealed this incident in the Quran to the Prophet.
- This comforted him, as he was sure there was nothing wrong with the message or his preaching.
- It was the hard-heartedness (the refusal to listen) of the leaders of Quraysh that kept the people away from this message.

Lessons Learned

- Prophet Muhammad never took revenge on anyone in his entire life, although many people persecuted him.
- For societal change, leaders must be approached first because they drive it.
- Our job is to deliver the right message; it is up to people to accept or reject it.
- Seeking the help of Allah in this effort is desired.
- Jinns are like human beings who understand Allah's unity and have a sense of good and evil.
- Allah does not leave His Prophets in difficult times.

story 4

The Opening of Makkah

Opening of Makkah

- While in Makkah, the Prophet and the Muslims went through a challenging time due to oppressive behavior from Quraysh leaders.

- Muslims, especially the slaves and poor, were tortured in the blazing sun.
- They were abused emotionally.
- Families boycotted their family members.
- Ultimately, the Quraish planned to kill Prophet Muhammad.
- Allah asked the Prophet and his companions to leave Makkah and migrate to Medinah.

- The Prophet and the Muslims were tested by leaving their homeland and families and migrating to a foreign land.

- When Muslims gained power in Mecca and the Makkans breached many peace contracts, Allah asked the Prophet to open Mecca for Islam.
- An army of more than 10000 Muslims planned to take over Makkah and punish Quraish.
- The leaders of the Quraish realized that Muslims would crush them today.
- They decided to lay down their arms and let Muslims come to Makkah without a fight.
- Their main leader, Abu Sufyan, was worried because he had fought many battles with Muslims.
- Finally, Prophet Muhammad ordered the army to enter Makkah.

- This was the perfect opportunity to take revenge on the people who threw Muslims out of their land.
- The Muslim army gave the impression that they would crush Quraysh, and no one would be spared.

- Abu Sufyan got worried. The Prophet reassured him with a surprising response: *"This is the day of kindness; today, the sanctity of the Kabaah shall be restored. Today, God shall honor the Quraysh."*
- The Quraysh delegation, who had come to meet outside Makkah, was asked to enter first.
- A general amnesty (forgiveness) was announced for the people of Makkah if they did not fight.
- They are advised to remain inside their homes.

Strict Instructions given to the Muslim Army

1. Not to kill anyone or to be the first to use weapons – you can only defend yourself.

2. The entry into Makkah must be completely peaceful, with no bloodshed.

3. Respect the delegation of Quraysh, especially Abu Sufyan, and if someone comes under his protection, he/she must be protected.

4. All idols in Kabaah must be broken, and Kabaah must be cleaned for worshiping one Allah.

وَمَا أَرْسَلْنَاكَ إِلَّا رَحْمَةً لِلْعَالَمِينَ

[O Muhmmad], you have not been but a mercy to humanity.

- He asked: "What kind of treatment do you expect from me?" They said: "Brotherly treatment. You are a kind brother and the son of a kind brother".

- He said: "I say to you what my brother Prophet Yusuf had said to his brothers: There is no accusation upon you today, go! You are all free."

- He forgave everyone despite all the wrongs committed toward him.

- Many people in Makkah accepted Islam simply by observing the Prophet's beautiful gesture.

- Remember, Prophet Muhammad was not sent to take revenge or hurt people. His main responsibility is to bring people to Islam and guide them to lead lives that please Allah.

Lessons Learned

- People in power must be the most merciful people on earth because they should remember that there is one more powerful above them, Allah.

- Forgiveness is a quality of Allah. If we want Allah to forgive us for our shortcomings, then we should also let people's mistakes go.

- No war is allowed to take over lands or other people's wealth. War is allowed by Allah so we can protect other people from being wronged by powerful people or nations.

Learn a new story about Prophet Muhammad's character and share it with the class.

Chapter 30

The story of Worship

In this chapter, we will learn about the daily Salah we pray, the special Salah we pray in Ramadan called Taraweeh, and the worship of Fasting.

The Story of Salah

History of Salah

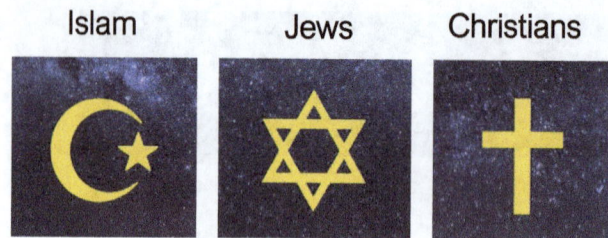

Islam   Jews   Christians

- Prayer or Salah is as old as the religion, from the time of Adam.
- All Prophets and their follower used to pray. Prophet Muhammad did not start Salah.
- The Quran mentions the following prophets who prayed: Ibrahim, Ismail, Shoaib, Ishaq, Yaqub, Musa, Zakariah, and Isa.
- The Quran mentioned that Jews and Christians used to pray. The Bible mentions Jesus's prayers.
- When the Quran asked Muslims to pray, they never found it a strange concept.
- The concept of prayers, in some form, exists in almost every religion, even man-made religions.

Why do we pray?

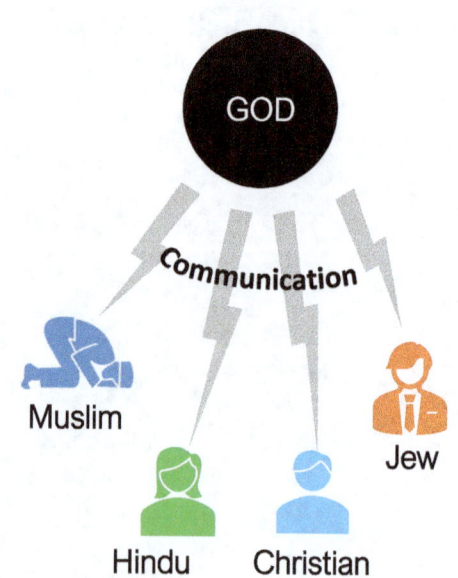

- In every religion, prayers are used to communicate with God.
- In the Quran, Allah told us to perform Salah regularly to **remember Him**.
- That is the best way to keep Allah in your daily life.
- People who do not do their Salah regularly forget Allah, who created them and gave them all the blessings they have.
- In a Muslim society, Salah is used as an identity to differentiate between a Muslim and a non-Muslim.
- Praying five times a day helps keep a check on our behavior and actions.
- It reminds us that the way we face Allah in every Salah, we will face Allah on the Day of Judgment.

Benefits of Salah

- The benefits of Salah can only be understood by those who regularly perform their Salah.
- It keeps us connected to Allah at all times.
- It keeps a check on us at least five times a day.
- It erases the sins we incur for disobeying Allah.
- It gives us the opportunity to seek Allah's help when we need it.
- It helps us in going through hardships.
- It's a way to thank Allah for His blessings.
- It keeps our faith strong when we feel down.
- Every creation of Allah praises Him, and by performing Salah, we also join them.
- It keeps our hearts clean of ills such as jealousy, envy, and hatred.

Hadith

Abu Huraira reported: The Messenger of Allah said, "If there was a river in front of your house and you took a bath in it five times a day, would you notice any dirt on yourself?" They said, "Not a trace of dirt would be left." The Prophet said, "That is the parable of the five prayers by which Allah removes sins and keeps you clean." [Sahih Al Bukhari #528]

How do we pray?

- Below is the method of how we pray.
- The best way to learn the method of Salah is to do it with our elders.

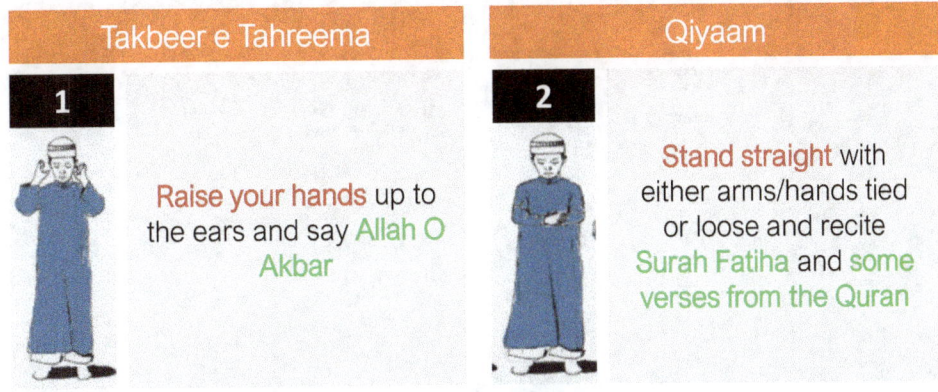

Takbeer e Tahreema	Qiyaam
1 Raise your hands up to the ears and say Allah O Akbar	**2** Stand straight with either arms/hands tied or loose and recite Surah Fatiha and some verses from the Quran

Rukoo	Qawmah
3	**4**

Rukoo — **3**

Say "Allah O Akbar" and bend your body while keeping your legs, arms, and back straight. Say Subhana Rabbial Azeem three times

Qawmah — **4**

Stand up straight again while saying Sami Allah O Liman Hamida Rabbana wa Lakal Hamd

Sajdah — **5**

Go in the position of Prostration and say Subhana Rabbial Aalaa three times. Repeat it twice with short sitting in between *(this completes one Rakah).*

Qadaah / Tashahud / Salam — **6**

If we pray 2 Rakah, we sit after the Sajdah and do supplications (dua) until Salam is said on both sides. If we pray 4 Rakah, then we stand up again and sit again at the end of the 4th Rakah and say Salam on both sides.

How to improve Salah?

Not sure who ate all the cake. I got none. ✗

Next month, will I have saved $50 or more? Let me count. ✗

O' Allah, I need your help! ✓

I have a great idea for the playdate!! ✗

What is this picture on Ahmed's T-shirt? ✗

- Perform proper Wudu with the intention of praying.
- Dress properly.
- Do not play with your clothes, hair, or anything.
- Avoid talking, responding to others, looking around, or paying attention to what others are doing.
- Avoid thinking about other matters and concentrate on Salah.
- Listen to what the Imam is reading if you are praying with someone.
- Read a little louder if praying alone so you can hear yourself.
- Think of it as your opportunity to talk to Allah and ask for His help.

Lessons Learned

- If you want to stay in touch with Allah, who is the King of the kings, then Salah is our only opportunity to do that.
- Use Salah during the day to reflect on what you have done wrong and how to improve on it.
- If you want to remain on the right path and avoid evil, then begin by praying your Salah regularly.
- On the Day of Judgement, Allah will ask us about our Salah. If that is good, all other questions will be easy to answer.
- If we miss one or two Salah, let Shaytan not discourage you from making them up and starting to pray again. Remember, Allah loves those who come back.

The Story of Fasting

History of Fasting

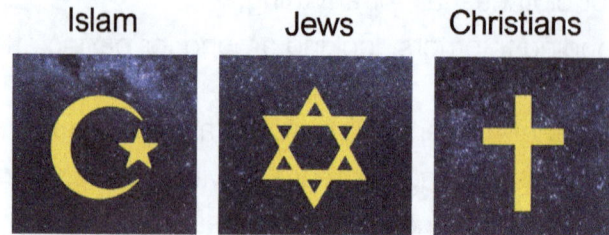

Islam   Jews   Christians

- The history of Fasting is the same as that of the Prayer and Zakah.
- The Quran stated that fasting was given to other nations before Muslims.
- The Arabs were aware of the term "Sawm".
- They used to fast on the 10th of Muharram.
- Christians and Jews also had this concept, and it is mentioned in the Bible.
- It reaches us through the Sunnah of the Prophet.
- Allah dedicated the month of Ramadan to fasting.

David pleaded with God for the child. He fasted, went into his house, and spent the nights lying on the ground. (Bible)

Why do we fast?

يا أَيُّهَا الَّذِينَ آمنوا كُتِبَ عَلَيْكُمُ الصِّيامُ كَمَا كُتِبَ عَلَى الَّذِينَ مِن قَبِلِكُم لَعَلَّكُم تَتَّقونَ

Believers! Fasting has been obligatory upon you as it was made obligatory upon those before you, so that you become God-conscious. (2:183)

- In the Arabic language, the word used for fasting is "Sawm," which means "to stop from something".
- The Quran stated the goal of fasting as "so that you become God-conscious" (called Taqwa).
- Having Taqwa means living within the limits set by God and remaining aware of Him in everything one does.
- Fasting creates obedience to Allah and patience in our personality.
- It teaches us how we can obey Allah if we want to – not that difficult.
- Prophet Muhammad has said: *Whoever fasts in Ramadan with the intention that he/she will continue to obey Allah after Ramadan, also, their past sins are forgiven by Allah.*

How to Fast?

- Fasting is required in the month of Ramadan.
- Ramadan begins with moonsighting.
- Fast from Fajr (before sunrise) to Nightfall (after sunset).
- Avoid the following during the fast:
  - Eating or drinking of any type.
  - Indecent talks or acts.
- If you skip fast during Ramadan for any reason, make up for it on other days.
- Intentionally breaking fast is a big sin.
- If you eat or drink forgetfully, then it does not break the fast.
- Optional fasting is allowed outside of Ramadan.

Don't miss the objective

- Fasting is a special time when we are supposed to engage in religious and positive activities, as we seek to get closer to Allah.
- However, most people miss the objective of fasting and engage in undesirable activities during the day.

Food fest   Lose temper

Watching movies   **Killing Time**   **Playing Cards**

Social media and Phone

Extra Salah   **Quran with translation**   **Islamic Books**

Charity Work

Lessons Learned

- Fasting in Ramadan is a period of training that helps us build patience and obedience.
- We should obey Allah the same way as we obey Him during Ramadan.
- We do not eat during Ramadan even when we are alone because we know He sees us – that is Taqwa.
- Ramadan is also a month of the Quran.
- Don't waste your time and take full advantage of fasting.
- It is an opportunity to get your past sins forgiven.

The Story of Taraweeh

What is Taraweeh?

Courtesy: Flikr

- This special Salah is prayed on the nights of Ramadan after Isha.
- In Arabic, Taraweeh means "Multiple Rests" because everyone rests briefly after 4 units of Salah.
- Muslims love this Salah and get together in the mosque every night to listen to the Quran.

Qiyam al Layl

- Allah instructed Prophet Muhammad to pray one additional night of Salah, called Qiyam ul Layl or Tahajjud.
- For this Salah, the Prophet must wake up in the middle of the night, and only odd-numbered units are prayed, such as 3, 5, 7, etc. That's why it's also called Witr (meaning odd number).
- In this Salah, the Quran is recited loudly in a medium pitch.
- The companions of the Prophet used to pray it just because Prophet Muhammad prayed it. However, for common Muslims, it is an optional Salah.
- Some companions of the Prophet loved this Salah and asked him for permission to pray it right after Isha, and he granted them permission. But its actual time was with Qiyam al-Layl (the third part of the night before Fajr).
- Today, most Muslims pray this Witr after Isha, which is the same as Tahajjud or Qiyam ul Layl.
- If someone wants to pray it according to the Sunnah of the Prophet Muhammad, they should wake up and pray it after midnight.

Prophet led Qiyam ul Layl

- On one night of Ramadan, the Prophet prayed Qiyam ul Layl in the mosque, and some people joined him.
- The next night, more people joined the Salah.

- After three nights, he did not come out, and people waited for him.
- He told them that he did not want this Salah to become mandatory for common Muslims, and that's why he stopped leading it.
- After this, people continued to pray it alone – some prayed in the middle of the night, and some prayed after Isha.

Taraweeh started

- When Omar Farooq was the Caliph of Muslims, one night of Ramadan, he visited the mosque after Isha.
- He found people performing Qiyam ul Layl or Tahajjud individually, and since everyone was reciting the Quran, the mosque was very noisy.
- He asked people why they don't appoint an Imam and pray together so everyone can enjoy this Salah.
- Since Omar was very disciplined, he brought that discipline to the optional Salah, which people loved to pray during Ramadan.
- Since then, people have prayed like this, especially during Ramadan, in the form of Taraweeh prayers.
- The name "Taraweeh" was adopted because it means "resting," and people take a short break after every four rakah due to the length of the recitation.
- Since this is an optional prayer for Muslims, they prayed in different units, such as 11, 23, 43, etc.
- There are no fixed units for this Salah as long as it is odd in number.
- In the old days, people used to pray up to 49 rakah for Taraweeh also.
- Today, most people pray either 11 or 23, including Witr.

Share your experience of Taraweeh with the class.

Activity Workbook

The Story of a Day of a Muslim Child

The Story of Ahmed & Aisha

- Muslims believe in Allah, and their day is different.
- We are asked to remember Allah at all times.
- Remembering Allah does not mean praying all the time.
- It means that Allah remains in our hearts and minds throughout the day.
- Prophet Muhammad taught us how to do it.
- We will learn all this in this story about Ahmed and Aisha spending their Friday.

Assignment

1. A daily prayer and dua sheet will be provided to each student.
2. Each student should manage their own sheet and update it every day with sincerity and honesty.

The day of Ahmad and Aisha

Early Rise

- Both Ahmed and Aisha wake up very early to perform their Fajr prayers.
- One of the wisest principles behind the five daily prayers is to build the habit of waking up early for Fajr.

- There are many health benefits of waking up early in the day, but they don't wake up for health benefits – they both wake up because Allah has asked Muslims to pray and remember Him through prayers.
- First thing: When Ahmed and Aisha open their eyes from sleep, the first thing they do is remember Allah by saying the beautiful dua that Prophet Muhammad taught us.

الحَمْدُ لِلّهِ الَّذِي أَحْيانا بَعْدَ ما أَماتَنا وَإِليه النُّشور

AlhamduLillah e alladhi Ahyana Ba'ada Ma Amatana Wa Ileyhin Nushoor

All praise is for Allah who gave us life after our death, and unto Him is the resurrection.

Going to the bathroom

- They always go to the bathroom first to freshen up.
- When using the bathroom, they both follow the following etiquette:
    - Say a dua before entering the bathroom (below-right).
    - Enter with the left foot first.
    - Avoid using mobile phones or any other devices while in the bathroom.
    - Use water to clean themselves, as this is the best way to follow the Prophet's sunnah.
    - Clean the area if required before they leave.
    - Say the dua as you leave the bathroom, with the right foot first (below-left).

Entering	اللّٰهُمَّ إِنِّي أَعوذُ بِكَ مِنَ الْخُبْثِ وَالْخَبَائِثِ
	Allahumma Inni Aaodhobika Minal Khubthe wal Khabaith
	O Allah, I take refuge with you from all evil and evil-doers.

Leaving	غُفْرَانَكَ
	Ghufranak
	I ask you (Allah) for forgiveness.

Making Wudu

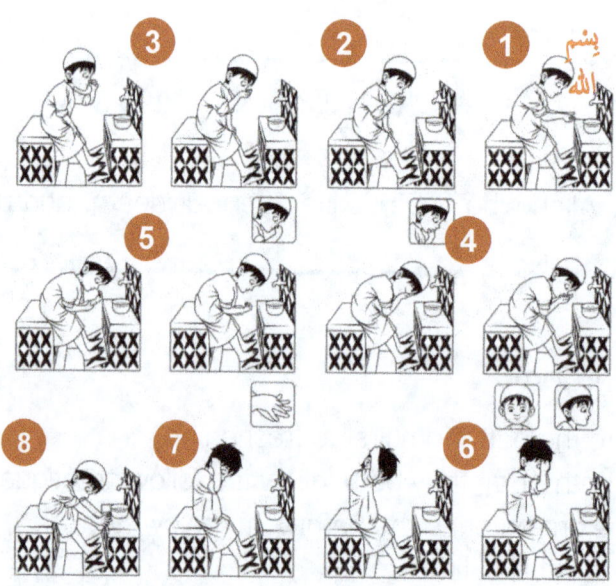

1. Start with *Bismillah* and wash your hands, beginning with the right hand.
2. Rinse your mouth thoroughly and brush your teeth, especially during Fajr.
3. Push water in the nose and clean it.
4. Wash your face, including the sides.
5. Wash both arms, starting with the right arm and working up to the elbow.
6. Wet your hands and wipe them on the head, going back and forth.
7. Wet your hands and clean your ears inside and out.
8. Wash both feet, starting with the right.

Duas of Wudu

Start	بِسْمِ الله
	Bismillah (In the name of Allah)

Finish	أَشْهَدُ أَنْ لَا إِلَهَ إِلَّا اللهُ وَحْدَهُ لَا شَرِيكَ لَهُ، وَأَشْهَدُ أَنَّ مُحَمَّداً عَبْدُهُ وَرَسُولُهُ
	Ash-hadu An Iaa Ilaaha Illallaahu Wahdahu Iaa Shareeka Iahu wa Ash-hadu Anna Muhammadan Abduhu wa Rasooluhu
	I bear witness that none has the right to be worshipped except Allah, Who has no partner, and I bear witness that Muhammad is His slave and His Messenger.

OR	اللَّهُمَّ اجْعَلْنِي مِنَ التَّوَّابِينَ وَاجْعَلْنِي مِنَ الْمُتَطَهِّرِينَ
	Allahumma Ja'alni Minat Tawwabeena wa Ja'alni Minal Mutatahireen
	O Allah, make me among those who turn to You in repentance and make me among those who are purified.

Importance of Cleanliness and Conservation of Water

- Prophet Muhammad once said, "Purification (Cleanliness) is half of faith."
- Purification in Islam is required in all things: our bodies, our food, our morals, and our hearts.
- Wudu and bathing keep our bodies clean.
- Allah loves cleanliness and pure people.
- When making wudu, do your best to conserve water.
- Prophet Muhammad used to perform wudu using only 1 *Mudd (2/3 of a liter) of water*.
- Check next time how much water you use when making wudu.

Assignment

Ask someone in your house to record a video of you while you are performing Wudu. Wudu must be performed as instructed, without wasting much water.

Praying Fajr Prayers

- Ahmed usually prays at a nearby mosque with his father, while Aisha prays with her mother at home.
- But since it was Friday, Aisha also wanted to pray in the mosque, so she decided to go with Ahmed.

- Prophet Muhammad encouraged everyone to pray in the mosque (men and women).
- There is no difference in the prayer method between men and women.
- However, praying in a congregation behind an Imam has different rules.
- Both were dressed well for the mosque, as it is recommended to dress appropriately when visiting the mosque (the house of Allah).

> Praying in the mosque is 25 times better than praying at home (Prophet Muhammad).

When starting a ride

- As Ahmed and Aisha were about to leave the house to sit in their father's car, Aisha reminded Ahmed that they had to recite the dua that they had learned from their father.
- Many bad things can happen outside, and only Allah can protect us.
- They also recited the dua before entering the mosque.

When Leaving the House

بِسْمِ اللهِ ، تَوَكَّلْتُ عَلَى اللهِ وَلا حَوْلَ وَلا قُوَّةَ إلاَّ بِالله

Bismillah, Tawakaltu Alal Lah, La Hawla Wala Quwwata illa Billah

In the name of Allah, I place my trust in Allah, and there is no might nor power except with Allah.

Entering the Mosque

اللّهُمَّ افْتَحْ لِي أَبْوابَ رَحْمَتِك

Allahummaftah Lee Abwaba Rahmatek

O Allah, open the gates of Your mercy for me.

Calling Adhan

- When Ahmed entered the mosque from the brother's Entrance, he noticed no one had called the Adhan for Fajr prayer. His father told him to call Adhan.
- This was his first time, so he was nervous, but he had always wanted to do that.

- He faced the Qibla and began calling Adhan, which he had learned from a friend.
- He knew that one had to beautify one's voice when reciting the Adhan.
- Putting one's hand(s) on ears is not required anymore because that was done in the old days to increase the reach of the call in the old days when there were no speakers.
- People listening to the Adhan should respond to its words and make dua in the end.

Wordings for Adhan

1 اَللّٰهُ اَكْبَر اَللّٰهُ اَكْبَر اَللّٰهُ اَكْبَر اَللّٰهُ اَكْبَر

Allahu Akbar   God is the Greatest

2 اَشْهَدُاَنْ لَّا اِلٰهَ اِلَّا الله   اَشْهَدُاَنْ لَّا اِلٰهَ اِلَّا الله

Ashhadu alla ilaha illallah   I bear witness that there is none worthy of worship except Allah

3 اَشْهَدُاَنْ مُحَمَّدًارَّسُولُ الله   اَشْهَدُاَنْ مُحَمَّدًارَّسُولُ الله

Ashhadu anna Muhammadar Rasulullah   I bear witness that Muhammad is the Messenger of Allah

4 حَيَّ عَلَى الصَّلٰوة حَيَّ عَلَى الصَّلٰوة   **5** حَيَّ عَلَى الْفَلَاح حَيَّ عَلَى الْفَلَاح

Hayya 'alal-Falah   Come to success   *Hayya 'alas-Salah*   Come to Prayer

6 اَلصَّلٰوةُ خَيْرٌ مِّنَ النَّوْمِ اَلصَّلٰوةُ خَيْرٌ مِّنَ النَّوْمِ   ← Only in Fajr

Assalatu khairum-minan-naum   Prayer is better than sleep

8 لَا اِلٰهَ اِلَّا الله   **7** اَللّٰهُ اَكْبَر اَللّٰهُ اَكْبَر

La ilaha illallah   There is none worthy of worship except Allah   *Allahu Akbar*   God is the Greatest

How to respond to Adhan

- Aisha was excited that Ahmed would give Adhan, but she also remembered that she had to respond to Adhan.
- She learned from her father that people listening to the Adhan should respond quietly, saying exactly what the caller says after each statement.
- For example, when the caller finishes saying, *Ashhadu alla ilaha illallah*, the listener should say *Ashhadu alla ilaha illallah* quietly.
- However, when the caller says *Hayya 'alas-Salah* and *Hayya alal Falah*, the listener should say "*La Hawla Wala Quwwata illa Billah*" (There is no might, no power except by Allah) each time.
- When the caller says *Assalatu khairum-minan-naum* in Fajr, the listener should say "*Sadaqta wa Bararta*" each time.
- Aisha followed the practice and responded to Adhan.

Dua after Adhan

- Ahmed and Aisha said the dua after Adhan. It is long, but they memorized it after hearing it so many times on TV.

اللَّهُمَّ رَبَّ هَذِهِ الدَّعْوَةِ التَّامَّةِ، وَالصَّلَاةِ الْقَائِمَةِ، آتِ مُحَمَّداً الْوَسِيلَةَ وَالْفَضِيلَةَ، وَابْعَثْهُ مَقَاماً مَحْمُوداً الَّذِي وَعَدْتَهُ.

'Allahumma Rabba hadhihid da`watit-tammah, was-salatil qa'imah, aati Muhammadan al-wasilata wal-fadilah, wa b`ath-hu maqaman mahmudan-il-ladhi wa`adtah'

O, Allah! The Lord of this perfect call and of the regular prayer which is about to establish, give Muhammad the right of intercession and favor and resurrect him to the best and the highest place in Paradise that You promised him.

Assignment

Students should call Adhan and demonstrate (both boys and girls). Listeners should respond, and everyone should read the dua at the end.

Praying two Rakah Sunnah

- After making Adhan, Ahmed and Aisha prayed two rakah (units) of Sunnah prayers for Fajr.

Saying Salam to the Mosque

- There is another Sunnah of Prophet Muhammad that Ahmad and Aisha forgot to follow, but it is highly recommended: praying two Rakah upon entering the mosque. It is called *Tahiyyat ul Masjid* (saying Salam to the mosque)
- If the person is already performing two Rakah Sunnah for Fajr or Zuhr, for example, that would also act as *Tahiyyat ul Masjid*.
- However, it is recommended to pray them separately.

- When it was time for the congregation, Ahmed was asked to call *Iqamah*.
- Iqamah is slightly different from Adhan.
- It is a sunnah that whoever says Adhan should say Iqamah also (but not necessary).
- Iqamah is a call to indicate that the prayer is about to start, and everyone should join.
- When Iqamah is called, we MUST leave everything and join the congregation – it is disrespectful to continue doing other things after Iqamah is called.
- In Iqamah, all statements must be said only once, with one exception. The exception is shown below. This must be added after *Hayya Al al Falah*.

قَدْ قَامَتِ ٱلصَّلَاةُ ۝ قَدْ قَامَتِ ٱلصَّلَاةُ ← Different from Adhan

Qad Qamatis-Salah

The prayer (Salah) has been established.

Note: Some Muslim Groups (Hanafis) repeat these statements twice, like in Adhan.

Assignment

Students should call Iqamah and demonstrate (both boys and girls). They can say the statements once or twice.

Prayer Method

- Prophet Muhammad said, "Pray as you see me praying." We try our best to pray as Prophet Muhammad used to pray.
- The best way to learn the method of Salah is to do it with our elders and follow them.

Takbeer e Tahreema	Qiyaam
1 Raise your hands up to your ears and say Allah O Akbar	**2** Stand straight with either arms/hands tied or loose and recite Surah Fatiha and some verses from the Quran

Rukoo	Qawmah
3 Say "Allah O Akbar" and bend your body while keeping your legs, arms, and back straight. Say Subhana Rabbial Azeem three times	**4** Stand up straight again while saying Sami Allah O Liman Hamida Rabbana wa Lakal Hamd

Note: This is a position to praise God. We can also say other statements of praise.

Sajdah	Qadaah / Tashahud / Salam
5 Go in the position of Prostration and say Subhana Rabbial Aalaa three times. Repeat it twice with short sitting in between *(this completes one Rakah).*	**6** If we pray 2 Rakah, we sit after the Sajdah and do supplications (dua) until Salam is said on both sides. If we pray 4 Rakah, then we stand up again and sit again at the end of the 4th Rakah and say Salam on both sides.

Note: This is a position to praise God and ask for Him. We can also say other statements of praise. Make lots of duas here.

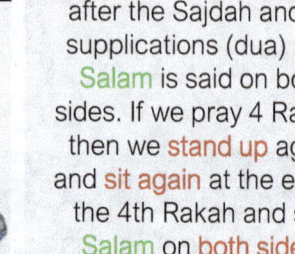

اَلسَّلَامُ عَلَيْكُمْ وَرَحْمَةُ اَللّٰهِ

Assalam O Alaikum Wa Rehmatullah

Duas in Sitting (Qadaah)

- In the sitting position before saying Salam, the following duas are recommended. However, it is a place for dua, and any dua can be made. This is your opportunity to make dua as much as possible before saying Salam. There are many duas reported from Prophet Muhammad. However, if you want to make dua in your language, then do so.

التَّحِيَّاتُ لِلهِ وَالصَّلَوَاتُ وَالطَّيِّبَاتُ، السَّلَامُ عَلَيْكَ أَيُّهَا النَّبِيُّ وَرَحْمَةُ اللهِ وَبَرَكَاتُهُ، السَّلَامُ عَلَيْنَا وَعَلَى عِبَادِ اللهِ الصَّالِحِينَ، أَشْهَدُ أَنْ لَا إِلَهَ إِلَّا اللهُ وَأَشْهَدُ أَنَّ مُحَمَّدًا عَبْدُهُ وَرَسُولُهُ

At-tahiyyatu Lillahi wa-salawatu wa't-tayyibat, as-salamu 'alayka ayyuha'n-Nabiyyu wa rahmat-Allahi wa barakatuhu. As-salamu 'alayna wa 'alaa 'ibad-Illah is-saliheen. ashhadu alla ilaha illallah wa ashhadu anna muhammadan 'abduhu wa rasuluhu

"All the best compliments, prayers, and good things are for Allah. Peace and Allah's Mercy and Blessings be on you, O Prophet! Peace be on the pious slaves of Allah and on us. I testify that none has the right to be worshipped but Allah, and I also testify that Muhammad is Allah's slave and His Apostle."

اللَّهُمَّ صَلِّ عَلَى مُحَمَّدٍ وَعَلَى آلِ مُحَمَّدٍ كَمَا صَلَّيْتَ عَلَى إِبْرَاهِيمَ وَعَلَى آلِ إِبْرَاهِيمَ إِنَّكَ حَمِيدٌ مَجِيدٌ اللَّهُمَّ بَارِكْ عَلَى مُحَمَّدٍ وَعَلَى آلِ مُحَمَّدٍ كَمَا بَارَكْتَ عَلَى إِبْرَاهِيمَ وَعَلَى آلِ إِبْرَاهِيمَ إِنَّكَ حَمِيدٌ مَجِيدٌ

Allāhumma ṣalli 'alā Muḥammadin wa 'alā āli Muḥammad(in), kamā ṣallayta 'alā Ibrāhīma wa 'alā āli Ibrāhīm(a), innaka Ḥamīdun Majīd. Allāhumma bārik 'alā Muḥammadin wa 'alā āli Muḥammad(in), kamā bārakta 'alā Ibrāhīma wa 'alā āli Ibrāhīm(a), innaka Ḥamīdun Majīd.

O Allah, send prayers upon Muhammad and the family of Muhammad just as You have sent prayers upon Ibrahim, and upon the family of Ibrahim, verily You are the Praiseworthy, the Glorious. O Allah, bless Muhammad and the family of Muhammad just as You have blessed Ibrahim and the family of Ibrahim. Verily, You are the praiseworthy and the glorious.

اللَّهُمَّ إِنِّي أَعُوذُ بِكَ مِنْ عَذَابِ القَبْرِ، وَمِنْ عَذَابِ جَهَنَّمَ، وَمِنْ فِتْنَةِ المَحْيَا وَالمَمَاتِ، وَمِنْ شَرِّ فِتْنَةِ المَسِيحِ الدَّجَّالِ

Allahumma Inni Aodhobika Min Adhabal Qabr, wamin Adhab-e-Jahannam, wamin Fitnatal Mahya wal Mammat wamin Sharri Fitnatal Maseeh Ad-Dajjal

O Allah, I take refuge in You from the punishment of the grave, from the torment of the Fire, from the trials and tribulations of life and death, and the evil affliction of Al-Maseeh Ad-Dajjal.

اللّهُمَّ إِنِّي ظَلَمْتُ نَفْسِي ظُلْماً كَثِيراً وَلا يَغْفِرُ الذُّنوبَ إِلاّ أَنْت ، فَاغْفِرْ لِي مَغْفِرَةً مِن عِنْدِكِ وَارْحَمْني، إِنَّكَ أَنْتَ الغَفورُ الرَّحيم

Allahumma Inni Zalamtu Nafsee Zulman Katheeran Wala Yaghfiruz zunooba illa Ant.
Faghfir lee Maghfiratan Min Indik Warhamni Innaka Antal Ghafoor ur Raheem

O Allah, I have indeed oppressed my soul excessively, and none can forgive sin except You, so forgive me a forgiveness from Yourself and have mercy upon me. Surely, You are the most forgiven and the most compassionate.

Adhkar after Salam

I ask Allah for forgiveness. (three times)   *Astaghfirullah*   أَسْتَغْفِرُ الله   **(Three Times)**   (1)

(2) اللّهُمَّ أَنْتَ السَّلامُ ، وَمِنْكَ السَّلام ، تَبَارَكْتَ يا ذا الجَلالِ وَالإِكْرام

Allahumma Antas Salam Wa Minkas Salam Tabarakta Ya Zaljalal e wal Ikram

O Allah, You are As-Salam, and from You is all peace; blessed are You, O Possessor of majesty and honor.

(3) لا إِلهَ إِلاّ الله وحدَهُ لا شريكَ لهُ، لهُ المُلْكُ ولهُ الحَمْد، وهوَ على كلّ شيءٍ قَدير، اللّهُمَّ لا مانِعَ لِما أَعْطَيْت، وَلا مُعْطِيَ لِما مَنَعْت، وَلا يَنْفَعُ ذا الجَدِّ مِنْكَ الجَد

La illaha Illallahu Wahdahu La Shareeka Lahu Lahul Mulk Wa Lahul Hamd Wa Hua Ala Kulli Shayen Qadeer. Allahumma La Mani'e Lima A'tayt, wala M'utee Lima Mana'at Wala Yanfao Zal Jad Minkal Jad

No one has the right to be worshipped except Allah without a partner. All sovereignty and praise belong to Him, and He is Omnipotent over all things. O Allah, none can prevent what You have willed to bestow, and none can bestow what You have willed to prevent, and no wealth or majesty can benefit anyone, as from You is all wealth and majesty.

الله أَكْبَر	الحَمْدُ لله	سُبْحانَ الله	(4)
Allah o Akbar	*AlhamduLillah*	*Subhanallah*	
33 Times	33 Times	33 Times	

(5) لا إِلهَ إِلاّ الله وَحْدَهُ لا شريكَ لَهُ، لهُ الملكُ ولهُ الحَمْد، وهُوَ على كُلّ شيءٍ قَدير

La illaha Illallahu Wahdahu La Shareeka Lahu Lahul Mulk Wa Lahul Hamd Wa Hua Ala Kulli Shayen Qadeer

No one has the right to be worshipped except Allah without a partner. All sovereignty and praise belong to Him, and He is Omnipotent over all things.

Praying in Congregation

Imam	Follower

1 — Says Allah O Akbar | Follows and says Allah O Akbar

2 — Recites Fatiha and Quran quietly during Zuhr and Asr and loudly in others | Recites Fatiha and Quran quietly during Zuhr and Asr, and remains quiet for others and listens to the Quran.

3 — Says Allah O Akbar and performs Ruku | Follows Imam and performs Ruku

4 — Says Samee Allah u Liman Hamidah | Follows Imam and says Rabbana Wa Lakal Hamd

5 — Says Allah O Akbar and performs Sajdah (twice) | Follows and performs Sajdah (twice)

6 — Says Allah O Akbar and sit and complete Salah and Say Salam on both sides. | Follows, sits, and completes Salah and Say Salam on both sides.

Do **not** compete with the Imam in action, and try to get ahead of him. The followers must follow the Imam.

Importance of Fajr Prayers

- Fajr prayers are special and carry the greatest reward among all prayers.
- It is difficult for most people to pray Fajr, but not for those who have a firm belief in Allah SWT and understand the reward of Fajr prayers.
- It is reported that Prophet Muhammad said that whoever prays Isha and Fajr with the congregation will receive the reward for praying the whole night.
- The Imam usually recites longer surahs in Fajr.
- According to the Quran, it is witnessed directly by Angels.
- Praying Fajr is the best way to start your day.
- It should be prayed earlier.
- It is prayed as 2 units of Sunnah and 2 units of Fard.

Etiquette of Mosques

- Mosques are houses of Allah, but Allah does not live there. When people visit the mosque, Allah treats them like His guests.
- We must always be respectful of mosques and people praying there.
- Pray 2 Rakah upon entering the mosque before sitting. This is called "*Tahiyyat ul Masjid*".
- When using the bathroom or Wudu area, clean the immediate area after using it – it is a public place, and everyone is responsible for keeping it clean.
- When Iqamah is made, join Salah as quickly as possible. It is better to be in the prayer area before Salah starts.
- Allow elders to take the front rows.
- People come here to pray and remember Allah, so do not make noise, especially in the prayer area.
- Socialize with your friends outside of the prayer area.
- Keep it clean and help when needed.
- When Adhan is made, stop everything and respond to Adhan.
- There are many volunteer needs at the mosque. Try to help as much as possible because this is a community place, run and maintained by the community.

Going back home

- Ahmed and Aisha enjoyed praying Fajr in the mosque – what a good way to start the day!
- Since they had school, they left the mosque to go back home.
- Their father reminded them to say a dua before leaving the mosque, sitting in the car, and entering the house.
- Now they were realizing what it meant to remember Allah at all times.

When Leaving the Mosque

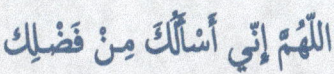

اللَّهُمَّ إِنِّي أَسْأَلُكَ مِنْ فَضْلِكَ

Allahumma Inni As'aluka Min Fadlik

O Allah, I ask You for Your blessings and favors.

Entering the House

بِسْمِ اللهِ وَلَجْنَا، وَبِسْمِ اللهِ خَرَجْنَا، وَعَلَى رَبِّنَا تَوَكَّلْنَا

Bismillah e Walajna Bismillah e Kharajna Wa Ala Rabbena Tawakkalna

In the name of Allah, we enter; in the name of Allah, we leave, and upon our Lord, we place our trust.

It's Breakfast Time

- We receive many blessings from Allah, and food is one of the greatest.
- Aisha has noticed that some people do not appreciate that, AlhamduLillah, they have plenty of food at their homes, while many people in different parts of the world are starving.
- Their parents ask Ahmed and Aisha to remember the following when eating food:

No Device, No Waste

- Remember Allah
- Thank Allah
- No Waste
- No devices

Duas for eating

If one remembers in the middle	Starting
بِسْمِ اللهِ في أَوَّلِهِ وَآخِرِهِ.	بِسْمِ اللهِ
Bismillah Fee Awwalihee wa Aakhirihee	*Bismillah*
In the name of Allah, in the beginning and the end.	In the name of Allah.

Finishing

الْحَمْدُ للهِ الَّذِي أَطْعَمَني هَذَا وَرَزَقْنيهِ مِنْ غَيْرِ حَوْلٍ مِنِّي وَلا قُوَّةٍ.

Alhamdulillah el Ladhi At'amni Haadha Wa Razaqneehee Min Ghairee Haulin Minnee Wala Quwwah

All praise is for Allah, who fed me this and provided it for me without any might or power from myself.

New Dress

- Another reason Aisha is excited today is that her mother bought her a new dress, and she decided to wear it for the first time on Friday.
- She remembers that every time she gets a new dress, her mother reminds her how grateful they should be to Allah, who provides everything for them without asking for anything.
- She asked her mother how she could be grateful and learn a dua for it.

Wearing a new dress

الحَمْدُ للهِ الَّذي كَساني هذا (الثَّوب) وَرَزَقَنيه مِنْ غَيْرِ حَولٍ مِنّي وَلا قوّة

Alhamdu lillahil-ladhee kasanee hadha (aththawb) warazaqaneehi min ghayri hawlin minnee wala quwwah

All Praise and Thanks are due to Allah, who has clothed me with this garment and provided it for me, with no power nor might from myself.

Its time to learn

- Ahmed and Aisha love their school and enjoy their friends' company while learning.
- They are always on time when going to school or doing anything because time is precious, and they understand its value.
- In Islam, many prayers are performed at specific times to be punctual.
- Five daily Salah, Fasting, Hajj, and Zakah are all done at specific times.
- They always pay attention to what teachers are teaching because they want to use their class time as efficiently as possible.
- This also allows them to excel in their studies.
- It's all because they value TIME.

Dua to increase in knowledge

رَبِّ زِدْنِي عِلْمًا

Rabbi Zidnee iLman

My Lord, increase me in knowledge.

Be nice to everyone!!

- Everyone at school loves Ahmed and Aisha because of their beautiful nature.
- They respect and love their teachers and friends, Muslims and Non-Muslims.
- They are always ready to listen to people, even when they do not agree with them on everything.
- They are always truthful when dealing with teachers and friends.
- They help their friends with classwork and homework.
- Some of their close friends are also very nice people because they are always careful in choosing friends.

It is **NOT** cool to be disrespectful to anyone!

Friday Prayers

- It is Friday, and Ahmad and Aisha have special permission from the school to take a break from classes to perform Jumuah prayers. This replaces Zuhr.
- Jumuah (Friday) is a special day for Muslims, like a small Eid.
- Muslims get together in large places like big mosques or conference centers (and sometimes a church rented for Jumuah)
- The father of Ahmad and Aisha picked them up from their school on the way to Jumuah.
- They are both excited to meet their friends, and today, the Khatib (the person who delivers the Friday sermon) is their favorite.
- Muslims hold Friday prayers to receive a reminder, at least once a week, of Allah and the guidance He has provided us for our lives.
- Friday Prayers (Jumuah) must be prayed in a central, larger place that can accommodate many Muslims.

Friday Practices (Recommended)

1   Read as much Durood as possible (Making Dua for the Prophet)

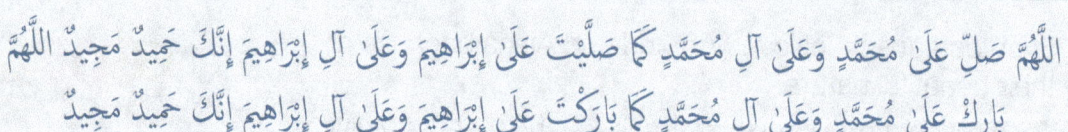

O Allah, send prayers upon Muhammad and the family of Muhammad just as You have sent prayers upon Ibrahim, and upon the family of Ibrahim, verily You are the Praiseworthy, the Glorious. O Allah, bless Muhammad and the family of Muhammad just as You have blessed Ibrahim and the family of Ibrahim. Verily, You are the praiseworthy and the glorious.

2   Read Surah Kahaf   

How Jumuah is prayed?

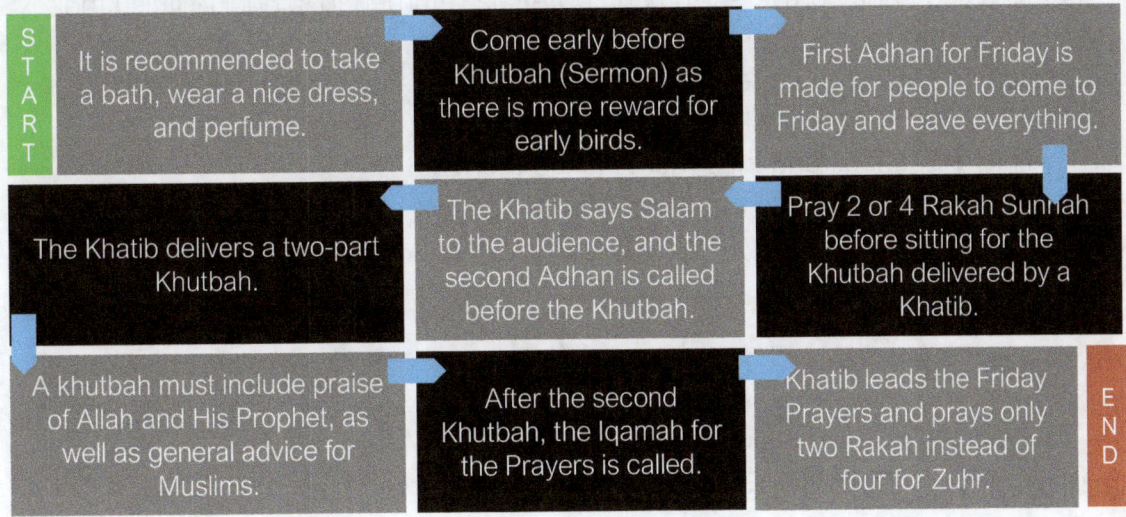

START → It is recommended to take a bath, wear a nice dress, and perfume. → Come early before Khutbah (Sermon) as there is more reward for early birds. → First Adhan for Friday is made for people to come to Friday and leave everything. → Pray 2 or 4 Rakah Sunnah before sitting for the Khutbah delivered by a Khatib. → The Khatib says Salam to the audience, and the second Adhan is called before the Khutbah. → The Khatib delivers a two-part Khutbah. → A khutbah must include praise of Allah and His Prophet, as well as general advice for Muslims. → After the second Khutbah, the Iqamah for the Prayers is called. → Khatib leads the Friday Prayers and prays only two Rakah instead of four for Zuhr. → **END**

Etiquette of Khutbah

- Prophet Muhammad has told us how to conduct when sitting in the Jumuah prayers.
- Many people do not follow them and do not get the benefit of the Friday prayers.

No Talking	Phone Silent	No device use

Hadith of Prophet Muhammad

"There is a time on Friday at which Allah grants the request of any Muslim servant who, at this time, happens to be asking Allah for something while standing in Prayer".

Note: This moment is around the time when Khatib is there for the Khutbah.

Going back to School

- After finishing Friday prayers, Ahmed and Aisha returned to school to finish their classes for the day.
- At the same time, they were quite excited about the evening because their cousins were visiting them for the weekend.
- They finished school, and their mom picked them up.
- They remembered the dua that they should recite when riding in a vehicle and entering the house.

Do you remember them?

Back to home - Remember Allah

- We love our homes not because of the materials they're made of; we love them because of the people we live with.
- Ahmed and Aisha have learned from their uncle that the way Muslims remember Allah all the time is because we associate every good thing with Allah, and we always go back to Him.

Home
Sweet
Home

Being Grateful	When some good happens	For something to happen in the future
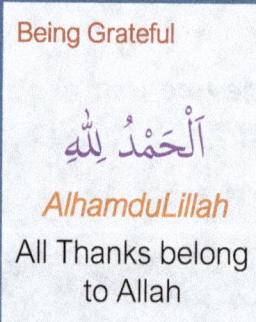	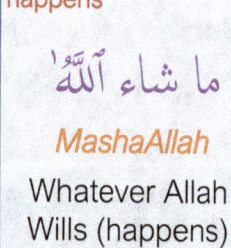	
AlhamduLillah	*MashaAllah*	*InshaAllah*
All Thanks belong to Allah	Whatever Allah Wills (happens)	If Allah wills, (it will happen)

Make it a practice to say

AlhamduLillah, **InshaAllah**, and *MashaAllah*

throughout the day. That is the best way to remember Allah at all times! However, it is important that you mean them, not just saying.

Spending time with family

- Even though Ahmed and Aisha are quite busy with their studies as they want to excel, they still make sure to spend time with their siblings and parents.
- They like to play video games and watch TV, but they realize that the time they spend on these activities isn't "quality time" because it doesn't benefit them much. They remember that their father always told them the difference between "using time" vs "killing time".
- The real quality time is what a person spends with their family.

Seeing the good and bad

- Sometimes people don't know what is good for them and what is bad for them just by looking at it.
- One day, Ahmed and Aisha asked their uncle about a Prophetic dua they should recite when they were unsure what was good for them.
- Their uncle taught them this dua that Prophet Muhammad used to make all the time, and they learned it immediately.

Asking Allah to show the good and the bad clearly

اَللّٰهُمَّ اَرِنَا الْحَقَّ حَقًّا وَّ ارْزُقْنَا اتِّبَاعَهُ وَ اَرِنَا الْبَاطِلَ بَاطِلًا وَّ ارْزُقْنَا اجْتِنَابَهُ

Allahumma arinal haqqa haqqaw warzuqnat tiba'ah, wa arinal baatila baatilaw warzuqnaj tinaabah

O Allah! Show us the truth as true, and help us to follow it. Show us falsehood for what it is and help us avoid it.

Falsehood → something that is based on a lie

Praying on Time

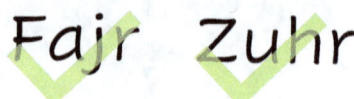

With all these activities going on, Ahmed and Aisha's family never forgets to pray on time. They always pray together as it is much better than praying alone.

Helping Parents

- Ahmed and Aisha are always very grateful to their parents for taking care of them, and they want to do something for them in return.
- However, since they are young, they do not know how to return the favors.
- Their father told them that at a young age, they could do two things to pay back:
  - By helping the parents with their daily chores.
  - By making dua for them.
- They learned this dua also from their parents, who always make it for their parents (their grandparents).

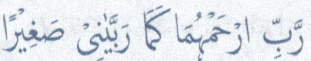

Rabbir hum Huma Kama Rabbayani Sagheera

Lord! be merciful to them the way they nursed me [with love and tenderness] in childhood."

Fun Time

- In Islam, we are asked to have a balance in life.
- That's why Ahmed and Aisha make sure to have some fun during the day, especially on weekends.
- However, they always spend their time in healthy, fun activities.
- They love playing basketball with their friends and swimming in their neighborhood pool.

Homework

- Ahmed had no homework from school, but Aisha had a lot of homework, and one of them was tough.
- Being a good student, she wanted to do it in the best possible way, but she was a little confused about how to do it.
- She decided to get help from her mother.
- Her mother not only helped her but also taught her a beautiful dua to ask Allah to make difficult things easy for her.
- She decided to memorize it over the weekend.

اللّهُمَّ لا سَهْلَ إلاَّ ما جَعَلْتَهُ سَهْلاً، وَأَنْتَ تَجْعَلُ الْحَزَنَ إذا شِئْتَ سَهْلاً.

Allahumma la sahla illa ma jaAAaltahu sahla, wa-anta tajAAalul hazana in shi'ta sahla.

O Allah, there is no ease except in that which You have made easy, and You make the difficulty, if You wish, easy.'

Quran study time

- Ahmed and Aisha's parents usually study the Quran as a family on Friday evening before dinner.
- This is a great opportunity for Ahmed and Aisha to study the Quran with their parents, learn how to read it properly, understand it, and ask questions.
- It is a great blessing for the entire family.

Hadith of Prophet Muhammad

Abu Huraira reported: The Prophet said, "Verily, Allah has caravans of angels who have no other work but to follow gatherings of Islamic study (remembering Allah). When they find such gatherings, they sit with them, and some of them surround the others with their wings until the space between them and the heavens is covered.

Dinner Time

- Ahmed and Aisha's parents gave them clear instructions to eat dinner together as a family.
- They both help their parents in doing final preparations and setting up the table.
- Their parents are always very grateful to Allah for providing everything to them. Ahmed and Aisha always hear their father making this dua before doing dinner:

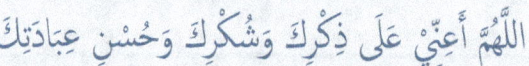

Allahumma A'inni ala dhikrika, wa shukrika, wa husni Ibadatika

O Allah! Help me remember You; be grateful to You; and worship You in an excellent manner.

• Wash hands	• Do not waste food
• Say *Bismillah*	• No electronic device or book
• Eat with right hand	• Say *AlhamduLillah* at the end
• Don't make chewing noises	• Wash hands
• Take what you can finish	

Before Sleeping

- Ahmed and Aisha wanted to go to bed early as their cousins will be visiting tomorrow and they planned a lot of activities with them. However, before going to bed, they make sure they have done the following:

- We are humans and we make mistakes throughout the day. Prophet Muhammad has taught us what to do when we displease Allah or a human being by committing a mistake.

- One of the practices that their grandfather taught them from one of the Sunnah's of Prophet Muhammad is constantly asking for forgiveness from Allah. This does not mean that a person says the statement of forgiveness with their tongue but it means to genuinely ask for forgiveness from Allah whenever they do something wrong with the intention to not repeat it.

- However, if a person has hurt someone, they must ask for forgiveness not only from Allah but also from the person who they have harmed and make up for the wrong. This is very important because on the day of judgment they will have to ask for forgiveness from the person who they have hurt. At that time, no one knows if that person would grant the forgiveness or not.

- It is said that Prophet Muhammad used to ask for forgiveness from Allah almost 70 times a day. Prophet Muhammad has taught us to say this statement:

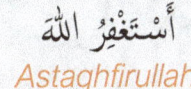

Astaghfirullah

I seek forgiveness from Allah.

- They also do a quick check on their day and how they spent it. What did they do right and what did they do wrong that should be avoided the next day. This is a great practice for someone to keep a check on their actions in front of Allah.

Etiquette of sleeping

- Ahmed and Aisha were tired after a long day. They realized that soon they would be dreaming.
- They always follow the sleeping etiquette their grandfather taught them.
- They avoid using any electronic device before sleeping

- They have memorized multiple Prophetic duas that they read before sleeping.
- Remember, they made a dua when they woke up. What a great blessing that they close their eyes remembering the name of Allah and open their eyes remembering Him.
- They always start by turning on their right side.

Duas before sleeping

بِاسْمِكَ اللَّهُمَّ أَمُوتُ وَأَحْيَا

Bismika Allaahumma 'amootu wa 'ahyaa.

In Your Name , O Allah , I die and I live.

اللَّهُمَّ إِنَّكَ خَلَقْتَ نَفْسِي وَأَنْتَ تَوَفَّاهَا لَكَ مَمَاتِهَا وَمَحْيَاهَا، إِنْ أَحْيَيْتَهَا فَاحْفَظْهَا، وَإِنْ أَمَتَّهَا فَاغْفِرْ لَهَا. اللَّهُمَّ إِنِّي أَسْأَلُكَ العَافِيَةَ.

Allahumma innaka khalaqta nafsee wa-anta tawaffaha, laka mamatuha wamahyaha in ahyaytaha fahfathha, wa-in amattaha faghfir laha. Allahumma innee as-alukal-AAafiyah.

O Allah, verily You have created my soul, and You shall take its life, to You belongs its life and death. If You should keep my soul alive, then protect it, and if You should take its life, then forgive it. O Allah, I ask You to grant me protection from evil.'